Big Feelings Devotions for Girls

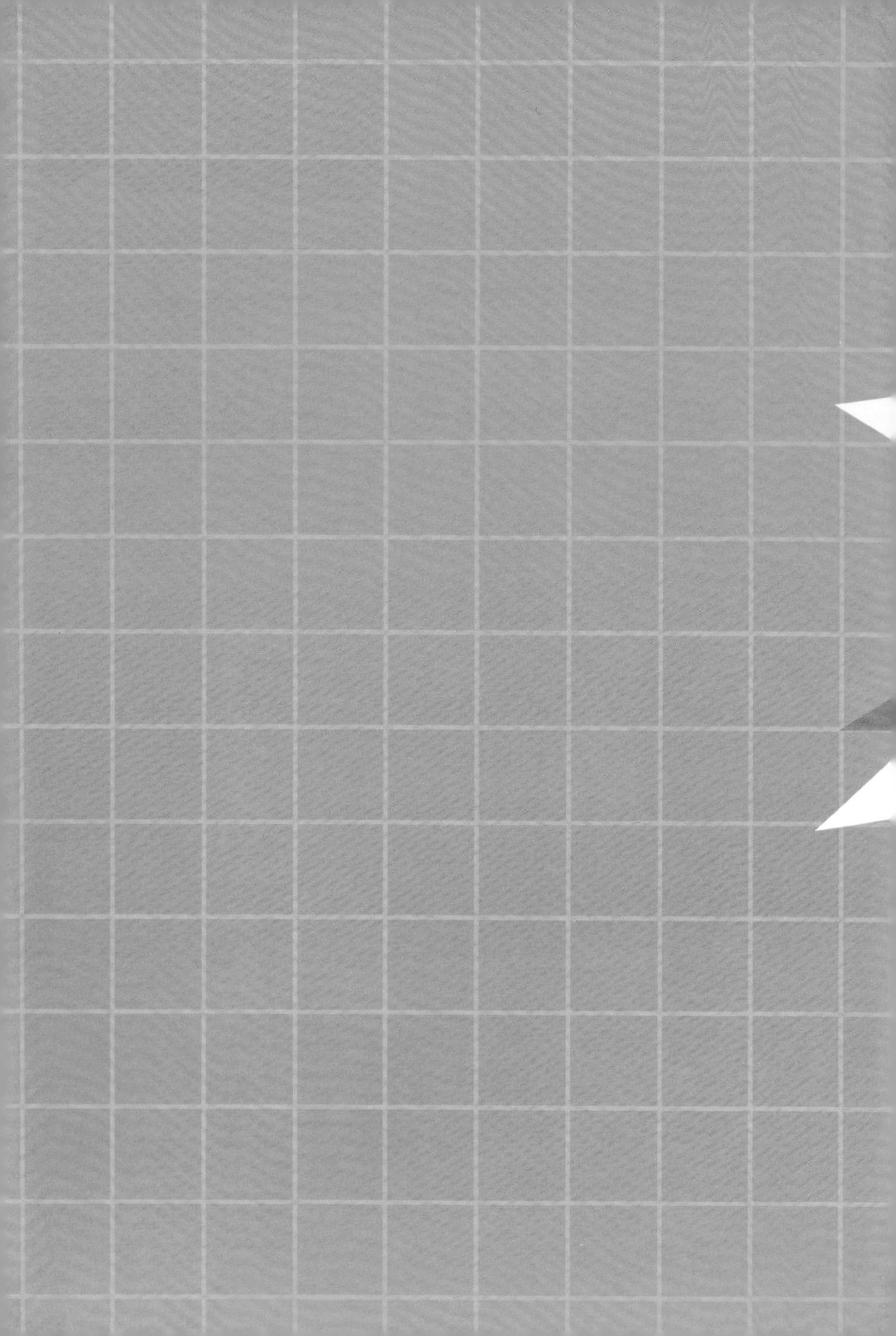

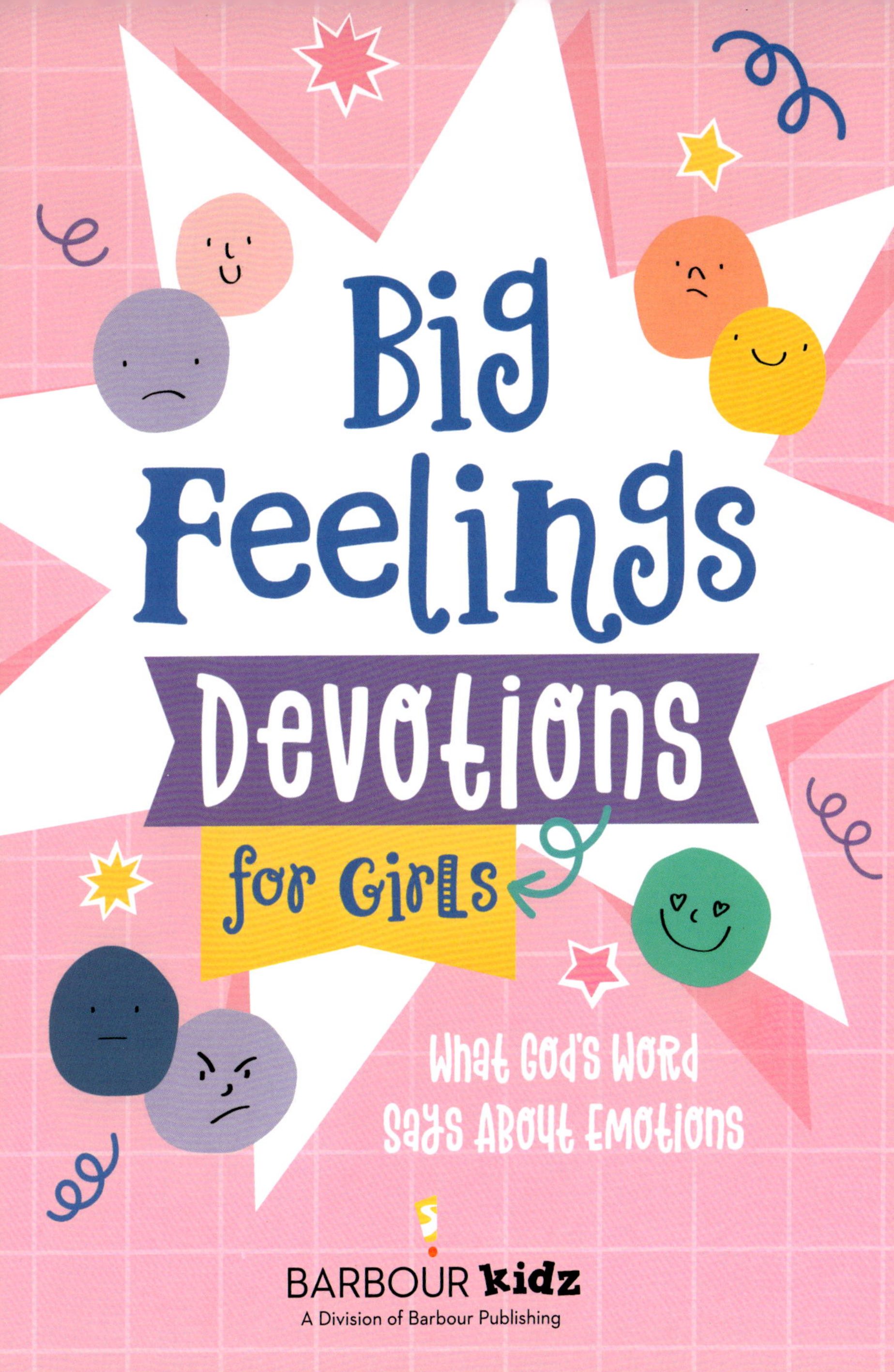
Big Feelings
Devotions
for Girls
What God's Word Says About Emotions
BARBOUR kidz
A Division of Barbour Publishing

YOU are the reason we do what we do here at Barbour Publishing. We promise that we will always use our God-given talents to produce content with you in mind—and that we will remain biblically faithful, no matter what.

Thank you for being the heart of our business.

Print ISBN 979-8-89151-254-2

Published by Barbour Publishing, Inc., 1810 Barbour Drive, Uhrichsville, Ohio 44683, www.barbourbooks.com

Our mission is to inspire the world with the life-changing message of the Bible.

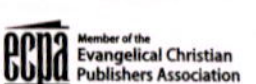

Printed in China.

002758 1225 HA

Introduction

You aren't a little girl anymore, but you aren't a teenager yet. These are your "tween" years. You are in between. You are experiencing more challenges than at any other time in your life. So much is new and so much is changing. As you change, your emotions change too. The tween years are filled with big feelings and so many moods. Anger. Sadness. Happiness. Fear. Frustration. Embarrassment. Anxiety. Joy. Confusion. Excitement. Hurt. Shame. Depression. Whatever you are feeling, *Big Feelings Devotions for Girls* will help. It will show you that God's Word is overflowing with wisdom and good advice to help you sort out your feelings and learn to understand and manage them.

How Are You Feeling?

Keep your minds thinking about things in heaven.
COLOSSIANS 3:2 NLV

How do you feel today? Are you happy, sad, excited, anxious? Maybe you can't describe your feelings. So much is changing and so much is happening that your feelings are upside down, mixed up, all over the place, and very, very *big*. Most girls your age have feelings that are hard to understand and describe. It's a part of growing up. The good thing is that God is bigger than all your feelings, and He knows exactly how you feel. When you talk with God and think about His words in the Bible, it can keep your feelings from getting too big and out of control. One way to connect with God is by thinking about and talking with Him all day long. If you feel anxious, worried, angry, or afraid, talking with God can help to calm you down. God is always with you and ready to help. Let's start with a prayer:

Dear God, I want to know You better.
I want to trust You with all my feelings so
You can help me sort them out. Amen.

Big Feelings

"The LORD your God. . .The Mighty One,
will save. . .He will quiet you with His love."
ZEPHANIAH 3:17 NKJV

Big feelings begin as little feelings. Think about blowing up a balloon. Little by little, air fills the balloon, and it gets bigger and bigger. Too much air and the balloon explodes. Feelings are like that. Imagine a guy watching a football game. He's happy when his team is winning, but when his team scores, that little bit of happiness grows into a big, excited, overjoyed feeling. It explodes when he claps and shouts, "Yeah!" Big feelings beg to be let out. It's fun to let out happy feelings because they explode into laughter, clapping, smiles, and cheers. Unhappy feelings, though, explode into big, ugly cries, angry meltdowns, worry, and fear. It is important to let those feelings out slowly so they won't explode. It's like letting air out of a balloon before it pops. God can help with that. He can quiet big, unhappy feelings with His love.

Dear God, I know You care for me and love me. Please teach me to let out my unhappy feelings before they get too big. Amen.

Hello, God. It's Me

For this reason, I bow my knees and pray to the Father.
EPHESIANS 3:14 NLV

When you were a little girl, maybe you were taught to kneel at bedtime and say your prayers. Kneeling is perfect because it shows respect for God. But did you know you can pray without kneeling anytime and anywhere? If your feelings get big and scary, wherever you are, you can tell God about it. He is listening all the time. Whether you are worried about something at school, afraid in a storm, angry with your brother for embarrassing you—whatever it is and however you feel, God wants to hear about it. Talking with Him can help your big feelings feel not so big. Get in the habit of talking with God all the time, either silently or aloud. Your heavenly Father hears your prayers. He loves you, and He wants all your feelings to be good.

It's me, God. Something is upsetting me, and I want to tell You about it. Talking with You helps me to calm down. It helps my feelings not to be so big and scary. Amen.

Good Thoughts, Good Feelings

Instead, they find happiness in the Teaching of the LORD, and they think about it day and night.

PSALM 1:2 CEV

God's Son, Jesus, is your best friend ever. Jesus is with you all the time, just like God is. When you talk with Jesus, it is like talking with God. You can imagine Jesus always by your side. When He lived on earth, Jesus had a lot to say about feelings. So did those who knew Him or followed His teaching. What they said about thoughts and feelings is written in the Bible's New Testament. If you read the Bible every day and think about what you read, it will set your thoughts in the right direction. Memorize this Bible verse: "Keep your minds thinking about whatever is true, whatever is respected, whatever is right, whatever is pure, whatever can be loved, and whatever is well thought of. If there is anything good and worth giving thanks for, think about these things" (Philippians 4:8 NLV). Thinking good thoughts leads to good feelings.

Dear Jesus, teach me to think good thoughts all day every day. Amen.

Write It Down

The thoughts of those who are right with God can be trusted.
PROVERBS 12:5 NLV

Thoughts often lead to feelings. A thought usually begins simple and small like, *I have a math test tomorrow*. If you're good at math and you've prepared for the test, you probably feel ready and relaxed. But if math is your most difficult subject and you haven't prepared, then you might feel worried and anxious. A single thought can make a feeling grow, and when worrisome feelings grow, they can become big and overwhelming. Forming a habit of writing about your feelings can help to sort them out and calm them down. Write from your heart as if you are writing to Jesus. Write not only about the big feelings that worry you but also about happy feelings. Someday you will look back at what you wrote and see how God worked everything out for good. Give it a try. Write down this prayer. Finish it using your own words:

Dear Jesus, right now, I am thinking about ________________, and I feel ________________.
[Add your own words to the prayer.] Amen.

I Feel Overwhelmed

So many people were coming and going that Jesus and the apostles did not even have a chance to eat. Then Jesus said, "Let's go to a place where we can be alone and get some rest."

MARK 6:31 CEV

There are many different feelings, and when several hit you all at once, they can send you spinning. One minute you're calm, the next you're frustrated, excited, horrified, relieved. . . All those feelings can lead to another feeling—overwhelmed. Jesus sometimes felt overwhelmed. Crowds wanting His attention followed Him all the time. When too much was going on, Jesus told His closest friends, "Let's go someplace quiet and rest for a while." Whenever you feel overwhelmed, you can imagine Jesus saying to you, "Let's go someplace quiet where we can be alone and rest." Resting with Jesus and talking with Him will help you unload your feelings and send them on their way.

Dear Jesus, way too much is going on right now. My feelings are all over the place. Let's find a quiet place to talk and rest. Amen.

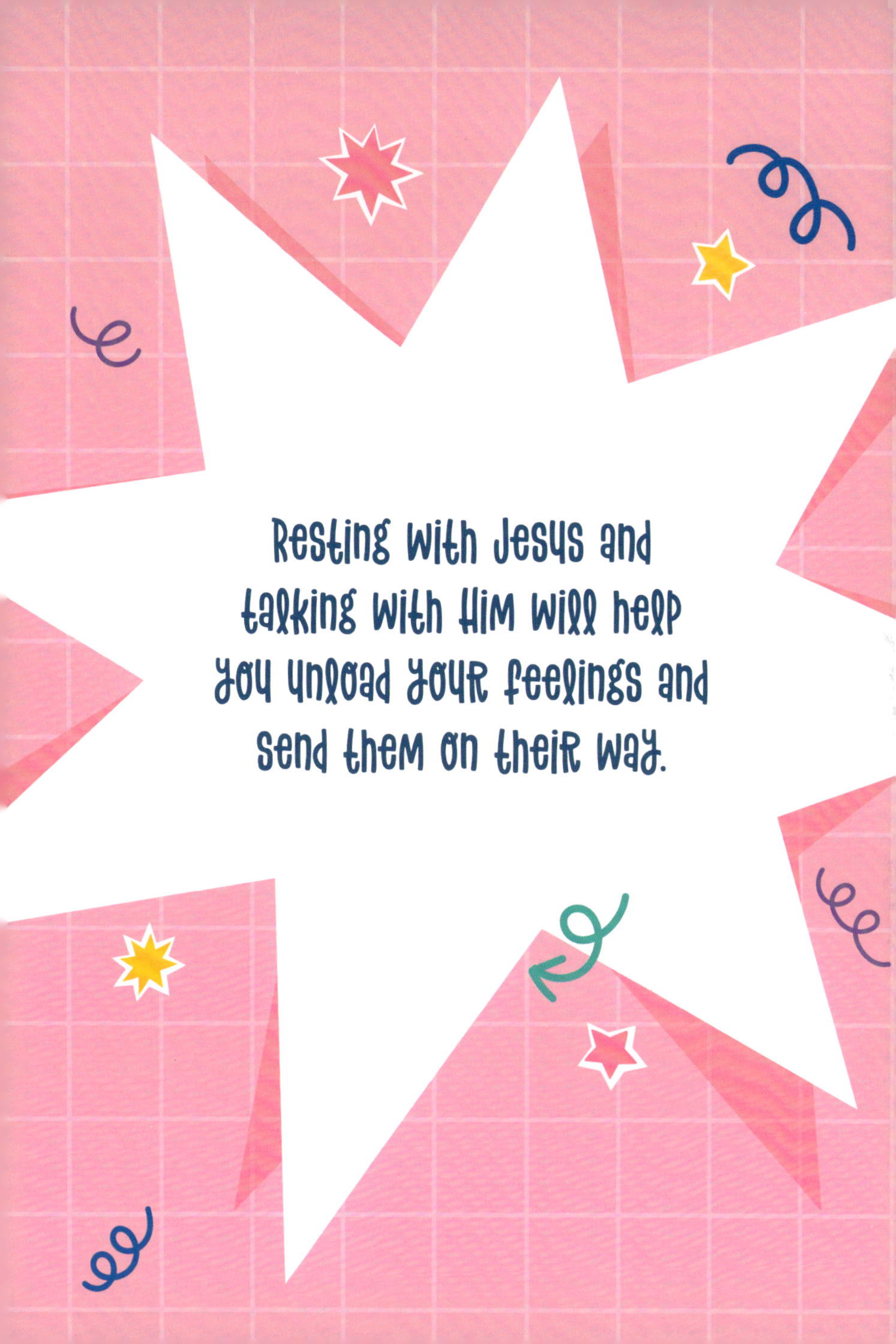
Resting with Jesus and
talking with Him will help
you unload your feelings and
send them on their way.

Patience, Dear

But those who wait on the LORD *shall renew their strength; they shall mount up with wings like eagles, they shall run and not be weary, they shall walk and not faint.*
ISAIAH 40:31 NKJV

"Just be patient." Kids hear that a lot. But patience isn't easy when something is bothering you. Sadness, worry, disappointment, and other unpleasant feelings might not turn around right away. It takes time. Patience means trusting in God and waiting for your feelings to change. While waiting, it's important to keep your thoughts set on Him, pray, and all the time believe that things will get better. When God asks you to wait, He could be teaching you to become more patient so you can build a stronger trust in Him. Isaiah 40:31 is another Bible verse to remember. It is God's promise to help when you feel like giving up and giving in to your feelings. Don't ever give up! Better days are coming. Believe it.

Waiting is hard, God. I'm doing my best to be patient, but I need Your help. Teach me to trust You even when my feelings don't change. Amen.

God's Perfect Timing

There is a special time for everything. There is a time for everything that happens under heaven.
ECCLESIASTES 3:1 NLV

Imagine a time when you felt anxious about something—a recital, starting a new school, trying something new, or even living away from home for a while—and then everything turned out better than you expected. Your anxious feelings went away, and you felt good again. God knows exactly when to turn your feelings around. When you feel worried and then you discover you had nothing to worry about, your trust in God increases. A wise king named Solomon noticed that God makes everything beautiful in His time. (Read it in the Bible in Ecclesiastes 3:11.) God's timing is different than ours. He doesn't change things when or how we expect. Instead, God works things out in His own time, His own way, and for our good. His timing is always perfect.

Heavenly Father, thank You for reminding me of times when You turned my bad feelings to good. I have faith now that You will do it for me again and again. Amen.

The Gloomies

So the Lord wants to show you kindness.
He waits on high to have loving-pity on you.
For the Lord is a God of what is right and fair.
And good will come to all those who hope in Him.
ISAIAH 30:18 NLV

If your art teacher asked you to paint a picture that defines the word *gloomy*, what would it look like? *Gloomy* is a word that reminds us of lonely places, dark and rainy days, sad songs. There is nothing good about gloomy. If you hold on to the gloomies too long, they can lead to another feeling—hopelessness. You don't want that feeling hanging around. God wants you to feel hopeful. That means looking forward to the future with optimism, believing that things will get better and everything will be all right. The Bible says that good comes to all who put their hope in God. You can trust God to turn things around. Just be patient and know that He wants to show you His loving-kindness.

Lord God, I don't want to feel gloomy or hopeless.
Help me to put my hope in You. Amen.

liar, liar!

"The devil has nothing to do with the truth. There is no truth in him. It is expected of the devil to lie, for he is a liar and the father of lies."
JOHN 8:44 NLV

Most girls want to be accepted. They want to be liked. Believing that nobody likes you or accepts you can lead to big, ugly feelings. God wants you to get rid of those feelings because they don't come from Him. They come from God's enemy, Satan. He is the biggest liar ever. Satan wants you to believe you don't matter when God says you *do* matter. Satan will do everything he can to make you feel like you're not good enough. Don't listen to his lies! God created you so He could love you, and whether you feel it or not, there are people in your life who love you too. Don't allow Satan to tell you otherwise.

God, if I feel that nobody likes me, I will turn to You because I know You love me. Please stop Satan from lying to me, and open my heart to all the love that surrounds me. Amen.

Wonderful Me

I praise you because of the wonderful way you created me.
PSALM 139:14 CEV

Some girls are envious of what other girls have. They want to be just as pretty or as popular. They want to be *that girl*. Envy is a feeling that can get you into trouble because it steers your thoughts away from God and His plans for you. God didn't make you exactly like someone else. He made you to be unique—special, one of a kind. He has a unique plan for your life too. God says, "For I know the plans I have for you. . .plans for well-being and not for trouble, to give you a future and a hope" (Jeremiah 29:11 NLV). It's okay to admire the good qualities in others, for example, their kindness, caring, and courage, and to desire more of those qualities for yourself, but you should be happy being who you are. Praise God for the wonderful way He made you. Trust that He is growing you into the girl He wants you to be.

Heavenly Father, I praise You for making me just as I am. Amen.

Imperfect Me

But now, O Lord, You are our Father.
We are the clay, and You are our pot maker.
All of us are the work of Your hand.
ISAIAH 64:8 NLV

Believing that you need to be perfect can make you feel anxious. The truth is that no one can be perfect, no one except God. He made humans to be less than perfect because imperfections give us room to learn and grow. Did you know that some artists deliberately reflect this in their art by adding a little flaw to their creations? It might be one missed stitch in a tapestry, a slightly different bead in a bracelet, or a tiny dent in a piece of pottery. They put it there to remind themselves and others that it is normal to be imperfect. God doesn't expect you to be perfect. He just wants you to do your best. It might not be perfect enough for you, but it is perfect enough for Him.

Dear God, I don't need to be perfect to please You. Thanks for making me a little imperfect so I'll have lots of room to grow. Amen.

1 PETER 3:4

Your beauty should come from the inside. It should come from the heart. This is the kind that lasts.

I Feel Pretty

Your beauty should come from the inside. It should come from the heart. This is the kind that lasts.
1 PETER 3:4 NLV

When Sophia looked in the mirror, she didn't see the beautiful girl God had created. Instead, she compared her looks to girls she saw in videos. Sophia convinced herself that her clothes weren't pretty, her hair wasn't pretty—she criticized her looks until she decided nothing about her was pretty. She worried that when others saw her, they would decide she wasn't pretty too. Sophia was listening to Satan's voice in her thoughts instead of God's. God was trying to tell Sophia that beauty comes from her heart. If she concentrated on all the great qualities that made her special, then when Sophia looked in the mirror, she would feel pretty. Her beauty on the inside would show in her sparkling eyes, her lovely smile, and her shining personality. Don't ever believe Satan's lies that you aren't pretty enough. God gave you a beautiful heart and a beautiful body too.

God, You gave me a beautiful, loving, caring heart. When I remember that, I feel pretty inside and out. Amen.

I Feel Confident

So do not throw away your confidence;
it will be richly rewarded.
HEBREWS 10:35 NIV

Confidence is a good feeling. It is a feeling that wants to grow big and strong. Confidence means believing in yourself and your abilities. It comes from putting your trust in God and in the strength He gives you to meet challenges. Confidence is comfortably stepping into a new experience willing to try and saying to yourself, "I've got this!" It's when you bravely walk into a room filled with kids you don't know and you look forward to making new friends. Confidence is trying again if you mess up. Remember—God is with you wherever you go, so you will never face your challenges alone. With each new experience, He will build your confidence, and as your confidence grows bigger, feelings like worry and fear will get smaller. Sometimes you will mess up. Everyone does. But never throw away your confidence. Keep on trying and believing that God will help you.

Dear Lord, will You please bless me with more confidence? I want to get better at facing new challenges calmly and with strength. Amen.

I Feel Determined

We must be determined to run the race that is ahead of us.
HEBREWS 12:1 CEV

Determination is another big feeling. It is believing that you can overcome any obstacle that gets in your way. It's being sure that God will guide you and lead you toward your goals. Gymnast Simone Biles is an example of someone who felt determined. Too much stress caused Simone to drop out of the 2020 Olympic games in Tokyo. It took courage to put her mental health ahead of the games, but she made the right choice. Simone needed to rest and feel better before she tried again. Her faith in God helped Simone stay determined. By 2024 she felt well enough to compete in the Paris Olympics, where she won her fifth gold medal and became the most decorated American gymnast ever. If something slows you down from reaching your goals, don't give up. Stay determined like Simone did. Then, whenever you're ready, try again.

God, when obstacles get in my way, I sometimes feel like giving up. Thank You for encouraging me to take a break and then keep on trying. Amen.

Stressed Out

"Come to Me, all of you who work and have heavy loads. I will give you rest."
MATTHEW 11:28 NLV

"Stressed out" is a really big feeling. Ali knew that feeling well. She tried to be perfect at everything she did—homework, ballet class, soccer, violin lessons. It was more than she could handle. She felt tired all the time, sad, and grumpy. When Ali's mom insisted that she drop all but one afterschool activity, Ali felt upset, disappointed, and even a little angry. But later she realized she had taken on too much. She needed a break. Stress is a feeling you must get rid of. If you allow stress to build up inside, it can explode into other unpleasant feelings. When you feel stressed out, talk about it with Jesus. Ask Him to guide you. He promises that if you come to Him, He will give you rest. Talk to your parents about it too.

Dear Jesus, too much of everything is coming at me, and I feel stressed out. Show me what to do. I need a break, and I need Your help. Amen.

Let It Out

[The wise words of the Proverbs] help you learn about the ways of wisdom and what is right and fair. They give. . .much learning and wisdom to those who are young.
PROVERBS 1:3–4 NLV

Something was bothering Olivia. Her mom knew because Olivia wasn't her usual self. "What's going on?" her mother asked. "Nothing," Olivia answered. She didn't like talking about her feelings. "Are you sure you don't want to talk about it?" asked her mom. Olivia's big, unhappy feelings burst out in a stream of tears. She told her mother about the huge argument she'd had with her best friend. Olivia's mom understood how she felt because she was once a girl Olivia's age. Her mom had experienced many of the same feelings, and she had wise advice for Olivia about what to do. Keeping big, unpleasant feelings bottled up inside isn't a good idea. It only allows those feelings to grow. When you talk with grown-ups about what's bothering you, they usually can help.

Father God, I know it's not good to hide unhappy feelings from my parents. Will You lead me to share my feelings with them so they can help me? Amen.

Hidden Feelings

Where can I go from Your Spirit?
Or where can I run away from where You are?
PSALM 139:7 NLV

Olivia felt ashamed. She had messed up and maybe lost her best friend. Olivia had told someone a secret her best friend told her. Soon that secret spread among the kids in their class. It ended with Olivia's best friend feeling angry and embarrassed and Olivia not knowing what to do. Olivia felt awful about what she had done, so awful that she tried hiding her feelings from God. The truth is that you can't hide anything from God. He sees and knows everything. If Olivia would pray and talk with God about what she had done, He would forgive her. He would also give Olivia courage to apologize to her friend and try to make things right. God still loves you when you mess up. You never have to be afraid to come to Him with your feelings, even when you feel embarrassed or ashamed.

Dear God, You saw what I did. I'm so ashamed. Please forgive me and help me to make things right again. Amen.

God Knows Me

You know when I sit down and when I get up. You understand my thoughts from far away.
PSALM 139:2 NLV

God thinks about you all the time. He knows you inside and out. He knows your DNA because He made you. God is like a GPS because He knows exactly where you are. God hears your words. He knows your thoughts, habits, strengths, weaknesses, hopes, dreams—everything! Maybe you feel uncomfortable knowing God is always watching you. He isn't watching you and waiting for you to mess up so He can punish you. Instead, God watches, guides, and protects you because He loves you. In Hebrews 13:5 (NLV) God promises, "I will never leave you or let you be alone." God keeps His promises. Throughout your whole life, He will be with you every minute of every day. Doesn't it feel good knowing that God is always with you, loving you and helping you?

Heavenly Father, knowing that I can count on You is comforting. Thank You for always being with me, watching over me, helping, and guiding me. Amen.

JOY

For You have made me glad by what You have done, O Lord. I will sing for joy at the works of Your hands.

PSALM 92:4 NLV

God blesses each of us with things we are good at. Mikayla was good with words. She loved discovering new words and learning how to spell them. Mikayla was happy when she won her class spelling bee and even happier when she won the all-city competition. Her happiness grew when she won the state regionals and then moved on to the state finals. In the finals, only Mikayla and one other girl were left. When Mikayla heard the winning word, her heart filled with joy. She knew how to spell it! It was the name of a bird that often visited her back yard. The other girl went first and spelled incorrectly. Then it was Mikayla's turn. "T-o-w-h-e-e!" Mikayla jumped up and down and clapped joyfully when the judge announced, "You won!" Joy is a big, happy feeling. Whenever you feel joyful for accomplishing something great, remember to thank God for making it possible.

Thank You, God, for this great thing I've accomplished. Thank You for filling my heart with joy. Amen.

PSALM 92:4

For You have made me glad by what You have done, O Lord. I will sing for joy at the works of Your hands.

I Feel Courageous

"Do not let your hearts be troubled or afraid."
JOHN 14:27 NLV

What do you imagine when you hear the word *courage*? A courageous act doesn't have to be daring and spectacular like saving people from a burning building or fighting a grizzly bear in the wild. It can be something as simple as standing up for yourself when others are against you or finding a path through obstacles that get in your way. Courage is a big feeling. It is so big that it has power over another big feeling—fear. Jesus says, "In the world you will have much trouble. But take hope! I have power over the world!" (John 16:33 NLV). Memorize that verse so that when you need some courage, it will help you remember that Jesus has power over every situation. He will help you to feel courageous and strong. Imagine a specific situation you might face that would require you to have courage. What would you do if you felt afraid?

Dear Jesus, when I feel afraid, I will remember that You are with me. You will help me to be courageous and strong. Amen.

God Will Protect Me

Be strong with the Lord's strength.
Put on the things God gives you to fight with.
EPHESIANS 6:10–11 NLV

The Bible gives us seven things to remember when we need to feel courageous and strong (Ephesians 6:10–18).

1. God gives us wisdom so we can tell truth from lies.
2. God teaches us right from wrong so we can fight fairly.
3. Trusting in God's power gives us peace even when we feel afraid.
4. Having faith in God makes us sure that He will protect us.
5. God's Son, Jesus, saves us from evil.
6. God's Word, the Bible, reminds us of God's promises and gives us strength.
7. Prayer allows us to ask God for help.

These things, when put together, are like a strong armor that protects us against fear. They remind us that God is our helper, and He will give us strength.

Father God, I need You. Please give me some of Your strength. Dress me in Your armor of protection. I have faith in You, and I trust You to help me. Amen.

What If?

Even if I walk through a very dark valley,
I will not be afraid, because you are with me.
PSALM 23:4 NCV

Luci worried, *What if something bad happens to someone I love? What if I fail my test? What if someone picks on me? What if. . .?* The what-ifs in Luci's mind shoved out the calm thoughts, and Luci felt afraid. Worrying made her forget that Jesus loves her, and He is always with her. Most of the time the things we worry about won't happen. But in those rare times when they do, Jesus promises to help us. As you get to know Jesus better, you will discover that you can always depend on Him. When you learn to trust Him, you will worry less about what might happen. Luci read Psalm 23 in her Bible. She memorized verse 4. Then, whenever the what-ifs showed up, she said the verse silently and chased them away.

Jesus, I want to replace my worries with thoughts of You. Remind me that most of what I worry about won't happen; but if it does, I will be okay because You are with me. Amen.

Discombobulated

Let your eyes look straight in front of you, and keep looking at what is in front of you. Watch the path of your feet, and all your ways will be sure.

PROVERBS 4:25–26 NLV

Discombobulated. It's a funny word but not a fun feeling. Discombobulated is the feeling we get when a bunch of little mess-ups happen all at once. Darcie almost missed the school bus; she forgot her lunch; when she got to class and opened her backpack, she couldn't find her homework; and then her tablet stopped working. She had trouble settling down and concentrating on her teacher's words. Darcie felt disorganized, confused—discombobulated! We all feel discombobulated sometimes. When it happens, we can ask God for help. Darcie took a deep breath. She silently asked God to help her calm down, to stop thinking about all that had gone wrong, and instead to concentrate on what was in front of her. With God's help, Darcie turned what had begun as a bad day into a better one.

Dear God, I feel so discombobulated today. Please help me to concentrate, to look forward and get back on track. Amen.

When we share an experience with others, it helps us understand their thoughts and feelings and to care even more.

I Understand

Be happy with those who are happy.
Be sad with those who are sad.
ROMANS 12:15 NLV

Empathy. It's a word that means understanding a person's situation and also their feelings. Zoe's friend had just learned that her parents were getting divorced. Zoe understood her friend's feelings because her parents had been divorced for several years. Zoe remembered that when her parents told her about their divorce, she felt sad, worried, angry, and even a little afraid of how things would change. Because Zoe remembered her feelings, she was able to understand how her friend felt and comfort her. Zoe had empathy for her friend. The Bible says, "Be happy with those who are happy. Be sad with those who are sad." When we share an experience with others, it helps us understand their thoughts and feelings and to care even more. Can you think of a situation when you felt empathy for someone?

God, please open my eyes to recognize when others are feeling an emotion that I have felt. Whether it's a happy feeling or a sad feeling, lead me to share that I understand how they feel. Amen.

Say What?

If there is someone whose faith is weak, be kind and receive him. Do not argue about what he thinks.
ROMANS 14:1 NLV

When someone accomplishes a goal and is happy, it's easy knowing what to say. "Good job!" "You did great!" "I'm so happy for you!" But it's not as easy to find the right words when someone feels sad, angry, or afraid. Empathy is good, but when you tell someone you know how they feel, choose your words carefully. It's best not to talk so much about yourself. Instead of explaining why you understand someone's feelings, you can simply say, "I think I know how you must feel. Do you want to talk about it?" Then be ready to listen without interrupting or giving advice. Remember—the other person's feelings are *their* feelings and not yours. They might not feel exactly as you did. If they don't want to talk about it, it will help just knowing that you are there for them and you care.

Lord, I want to learn how to show empathy. Teach me not only to understand someone's feelings but also what to say. Amen.

Surprise!

You won't be afraid of sudden trouble. . .
because the LORD will keep you safe.
He will keep you from being trapped.
PROVERBS 3:25–26 NCV

Chloe believed that she and her mom were just dropping off some packages at her aunt's house, but when they went inside—"Surprise!" Chloe's friends were there to celebrate her birthday. A rush of excitement raced through Chloe. Then, all at once, that feeling of surprise turned into a feeling of happiness. Surprise is the sudden rush we get when something unexpected happens. Surprise can shift to happiness, as it did for Chloe; but depending on the situation, it can also change to a not-so-good feeling. Imagine going for a walk and suddenly there in front of you is a wolf. Surprise! If trouble surprises you and then it shifts to fear, remember you aren't trapped in that scary feeling. God is with you, and He will keep you safe.

Jesus, if ever trouble comes suddenly and I feel afraid, I will remember that You are my helper. I will put my trust in You to lead me away from trouble and keep me safe. Amen.

I'm So Tired

Even children become tired and need to rest,
and young people trip and fall.
ISAIAH 40:30 NCV

Have you noticed that feelings can be big or little? You can feel a little afraid, or you can feel terrified; a little sad or heartbroken; a little upset or furious. Tired is another one of those little/big feelings. It is normal to feel a little sleepy at bedtime or to feel very tired after playing sports. It's not normal, though, to feel tired all the time. Worry and stress can make you feel tired. Sickness can make you feel tired. So can depression—feeling hopeless and sad all the time. If you feel tired a lot, tell your parents. Let them know when something bothers you physically or if you are worried or afraid. They will guide you toward feeling better so you can have energy to do well in school and have fun with your friends.

Dear Lord Jesus, I don't know what's going on with me that I feel tired all the time. But You do! Please help my parents and me to find out why I'm so tired so I can feel better. Amen.

I'm So Sad

Show me loving-kindness, O Lord. . . .
My eyes, my soul and my body are
becoming weak from being sad.
PSALM 31:9 NLV

Mia noticed a big change in her brother. He stayed in his room and slept a lot, and whenever Mia tried talking with him, he said, "Just leave me alone." Mia sensed that her brother was sad, not just a little but a lot. She wondered if her mom noticed. She was very busy with work and other things, and Mia didn't want to add to her troubles. But Mia decided it was right to tell her mom about the changes in her brother's behavior. It was good that she did. Depression often doesn't go away by itself. With help from a doctor and from God, Mia's brother let go of his big, unhappy feelings. If you know someone who is sad all the time, tell an adult. They will know where to find help for big feelings that get too big.

Dear God, it isn't right to feel sad all the time. If I or someone I know feels depressed, please lead us to the special kind of help we need. Amen.

Words Matter

Pleasing words are like honey. They are sweet to the soul and healing to the bones.
PROVERBS 16:24 NLV

Sometimes people lie because they don't want to hurt someone with the truth. It's good to care about how others feel, but still, lying isn't right. If you choose your words wisely, you can be honest without being hurtful. For example, if you want to go to the movies instead of visiting Grandma, you could say, "I love spending time with you, Grandma, but a friend invited me to the movies today. Can I visit you tomorrow?" If your aunt gave you a book you knew you wouldn't like, you could respond, "Thank you for the book! You know how much I love to read." If your friend messed up at her dance recital, you might say, "You tried really hard." If you think your words might hurt, don't lie. Do your best to say something positive. Think about what to say and ask God to help you.

Heavenly Father, teach me to be honest without hurting someone's feelings. Finding the right words is hard sometimes, but I know You will help me. Amen.

PROVERBS 16:24

Pleasing words are like honey. They are sweet to the soul and healing to the bones.

Totally Awesome!

For the LORD Most High is awesome,
the great King over all the earth.
PSALM 47:2 NIV

You are awesome! You know you are. There are many awesome things about you. You have special talents and skills. You have a lovely personality. You don't need to add to your awesomeness for your friends and family to love you and think you are awesome just as you are. So, what does *awe* mean? Awe is a strong feeling of respect and wonder when we experience or see something amazing. The Bible says our God is an awesome God. He is King of the earth and King of the universe. Everything God does is awesome. He knows what's going on with everything all the time. He has power over every situation. God created the oceans, mountains, sky, stars. . . Can you name other awesome things God created? One of them is *you*! God made you, and you are totally awesome in His sight. His love for you is awesome, and that will never change.

Dear God, everything You are and everything
You do is awesome. With great respect,
I praise and honor You. Amen.

I Adore You

Jesus said to him, "'You must love the Lord your God with all your heart and with all your soul and with all your mind.'"
MATTHEW 22:37 NLV

Every morning before Natalya left for school, her mom hugged her and said, "I adore you, honey." Natalya's mom preferred saying "I adore you" to "I love you" because her love for Natalya was so deep. Adoration is the deepest feeling of love. It is when you love someone or something more than you can describe. Jesus told us, "You must love the Lord your God with all your heart and with all your soul and with all your mind." He reminded us that our love for God should be deeper than the love we have for anyone or anything else. Everything God does, He does because He adores us. When you pray, tell God how much you love Him. As you praise Him and thank Him, your adoration for Him will grow.

O God, You are so great. Thank You for watching over me and caring for me. Thank You for guiding and helping me. Lord God, I love You so much. I adore You. Amen.

Sing a New Song

He put a new song in my mouth,
a song of praise to our God.
PSALM 40:3 NLV

Do you have a favorite song, one you enjoy singing aloud? Maybe, when you're quiet, you also hear it playing inside your head. Emma loved searching for new songs and discovering performers she hadn't heard of. Her friend introduced her to a streaming radio station that played the latest Christian worship and praise songs. Emma was surprised by the variety of songs and music styles she heard. She added some favorites to her playlist. Emma sang along to them, and sometimes she danced too. The music filled her heart with joy. The words of the songs helped Emma feel nearer to God and feel grateful to Him for all the wonderful things He does. Do you listen to Christian music? Give it a try. Maybe, like Emma, you will discover new songs to love.

Thank You, God, for creating music. Hearing it makes me feel happy and calms me down. Thank You for worship songs that fill my heart with thoughts of You. Amen.

I Feel Thankful

Always give thanks for all things to God the Father in the name of our Lord Jesus Christ.
EPHESIANS 5:20 NLV

Thanks is a word we often say, but sometimes it doesn't come with a true feeling of gratitude. Thankfulness is a feeling deep inside the heart that grows from appreciation. It is about the kindness of others. Thankfulness is a feeling we need to work at. It requires noticing and appreciating what God and others do for us. Try this: Think of all the little and big things you appreciate and are thankful for. As you list each thing, whisper, "Thank You, God." Get in the habit of doing this every day. When you make thanking God part of your routine, true thankfulness will grow inside your heart. God will help you see not only His kindness but the kindness of people all around you.

Dear God, forgive me for not thanking You for the normal everyday things—the air I breathe, sunshine, food, family, friends. . . Please make me aware of the goodness that surrounds me so my feeling of thankfulness will grow.

I Feel Appreciated

I am thankful to God all the time for you. I am thankful for the loving-favor God has given to you because you belong to Christ Jesus.
1 CORINTHIANS 1:4 NLV

Liz looked after her younger siblings when her mom was busy with work. To thank Liz, her mom took her on a special mother-daughter date. Liz felt appreciated and loved. There are many ways to show people that you feel grateful for the kind things they do. A thank-you note is a great way to show your appreciation. A gift you made is another way to show your gratefulness; so is spending time with someone doing something they love. First Corinthians 1:4 reminds us to thank others for their goodness and to thank God for the kind people He puts in our lives. Can you think of something someone said or did that made you feel appreciated? What are some things you can say and do to show your appreciation to others?

Lord, I'm grateful for family and friends who love me, help me, and are kind to me. Teach me to show I appreciate them. Amen.

Give it a Workout

I don't run without a goal. And I don't box by beating my fists in the air. I keep my body under control and make it my slave.

1 CORINTHIANS 9:26–27 CEV

Amelia's dad noticed her anxiety growing. "Come on," he said. "Let's go for a run." Amelia felt better after running with her dad. Running helped calm her feelings. As a bonus, it gave her one-on-one time with her dad to talk about how she felt and to hear his suggestions for other ways to calm down. Exercise, like running, is a great way to calm your feelings, especially when you feel angry or stressed. Exercise releases chemicals in the brain that can improve a bad mood. When you notice a big feeling getting too big, give it a workout. Do something physical. Use your body to get rid of that big, ugly mood.

Father, as I exercise my body, please clear my mind of worrisome thoughts. With each breath I take, I will praise You and remember that You are here, helping me and giving me peace. Amen.

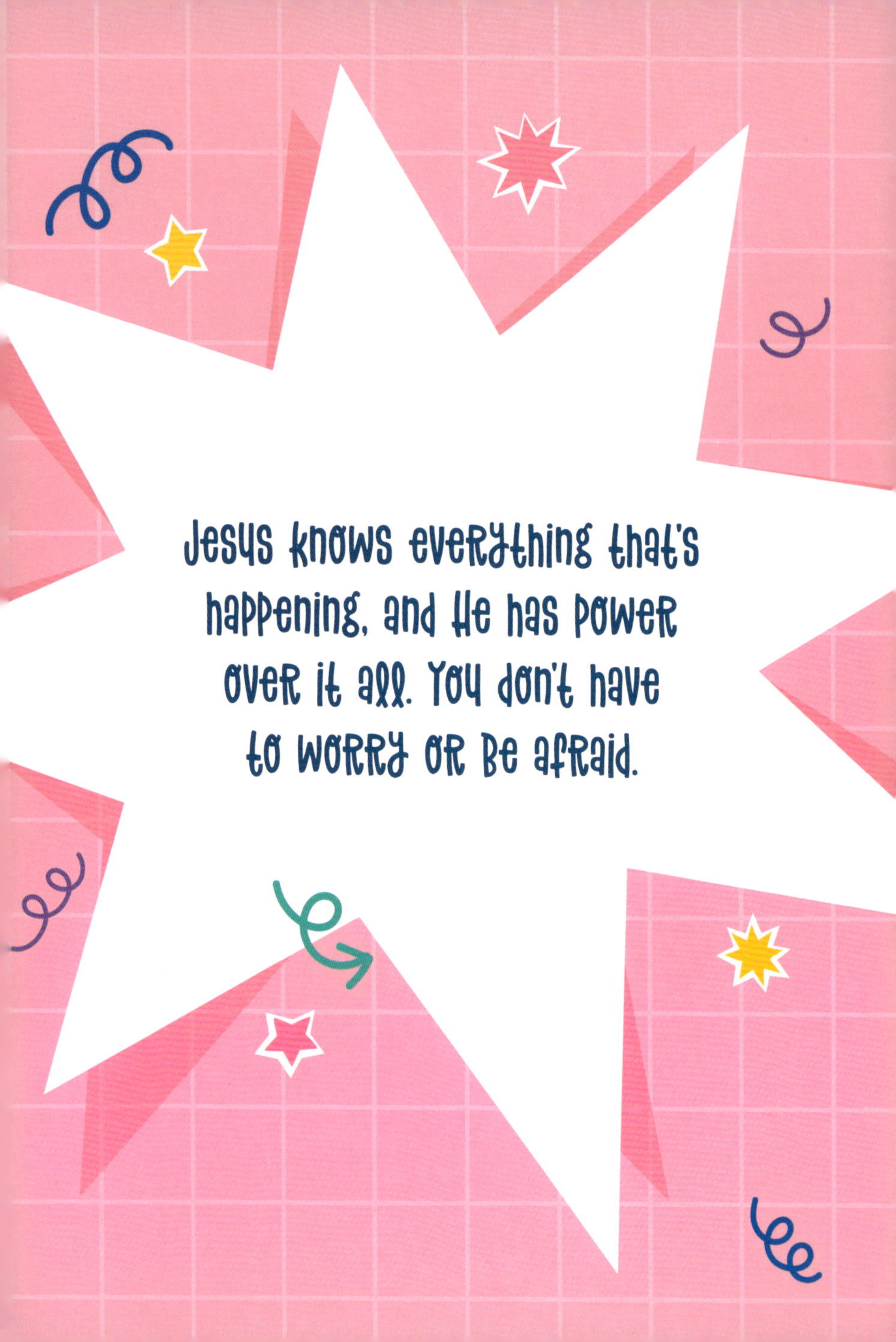
Jesus knows everything that's happening, and He has power over it all. You don't have to worry or be afraid.

[Jesus] answered [the Pharisees],
"You are from below. I am from above.
You are of this world. I am not of this world."
JOHN 8:23 NLV

The world is big, busy, and ever changing. The changes happen quickly, and all those rapid changes can make us feel anxious. The news we see and hear focuses on bad stuff that's happening, and maybe some of it makes you feel worried or afraid. Jesus said the world will always have trouble. People will always do things God doesn't approve of. But Jesus also said He has control of the world. Jesus knows everything that's happening, and He has power over it all. You don't have to worry or be afraid. Jesus will take care of everything in His own time and His own way. He will take care of you too. Ask Jesus to calm your thoughts and help you focus on the good things.

Lord Jesus, some of what's happening in the world scares me. It helps knowing that You have power over it all. Fill my mind with good thoughts and remind me that You will take care of me. Amen.

I Feel Anxious

Search me, God, and know my heart;
test me and know my anxious thoughts.
PSALM 139:23 NIV

Sometimes feelings mix together, and it's hard to find one word to express how we feel. Holly worried a lot about what might happen, she felt somewhat afraid, and she wasn't able to relax. At times, Holly felt her heart beat faster, and her stomach felt a little upset. A word to describe Holly's feelings is *anxiety*. It's normal to feel anxious sometimes. But when anxiety hangs on and grows bigger, that's not good. Maybe you don't know why you feel anxious, but God does. He knows all your feelings and how to untangle them. Talk with God about what's upsetting you. Tell Him how you feel. When your anxiety hangs around too long, tell your parents or another trusted adult. Ask them to help you find ways to get rid of all those mixed up, unpleasant feelings.

Heavenly Father, I'm feeling anxious, and I'm not sure why. So many things worry me, and I think a lot about bad things that might happen. Please, God, help me to feel better. Amen.

I Feel Excited

When [Rhoda] heard Peter's voice, she was too excited to open the gate. She ran back into the house and said Peter was standing there.

ACTS 12:14 CEV

Acts 12:1–17 tells about a man named Peter who was put in prison for preaching about Jesus. God made a way for Peter to escape, but when Peter returned to his friend's home, the gate was locked. He knocked, and when the servant girl Rhoda saw him standing there, she was so excited that instead of opening the gate for him, she ran inside and shouted, "Peter is here!" Have you been so excited about something that you couldn't wait to tell someone? Excitement is a big, happy feeling. You can be excited by something that has already happened or excited about something you hope will happen. What are you excited about? God wants your feelings of happiness to grow. He wants you to be excited about your life right now and excited about what you hope for.

Dear God, I feel excited about all the good things happening in my life, and I'm excited to find out what You have planned for my future. Amen.

God Has a Plan for Me

"'For I know the plans I have for you,' says the Lord, 'plans for well-being and not for trouble, to give you a future and a hope.'"
JEREMIAH 29:11 NLV

Lacey's oldest sister was in high school and facing some big decisions about her future. *What should she do after graduation? Work? Go to college? Something else?* One afternoon Lacey noticed her sister praying. Lacey asked, "What were you praying about?" Her sister answered, "I'm not sure what to do after graduation, so I was asking God about His plans for me." God has a plan for everyone. He wants us to stay away from trouble and have a future filled with goodness and hope. Lacey learned from her sister to feel hopeful about her future because God already had it planned. Do you have thoughts about what you would like to do when you grow up? God has a plan for you too. Pray about it and ask Him to lead you.

Lord, please guide me toward what You want for my future. I feel hopeful because my future is in Your hands, and Your plans for me are good. Amen.

Child of God

See what great love the Father has for us that He would call us His children. And that is what we are.
1 JOHN 3:1 NLV

Think about this question: *Who are you?* You can think of it as a simple question with a simple answer and say your name. But, really, it is a much bigger question. You are more than just your name. So, *who are you?* You are someone who is smart and who has special skills and talents. You are someone with feelings that make you happy and sometimes hurt. You might be a niece, a granddaughter, a cousin, a sister. . . You are your parents' daughter. And you are God's child. That's who you are—a child of God! He loves you so much that your heavenly Father, the one who created you, calls you His own. The love He feels for you is so big it can't be measured, and it will last forever. How does that make you feel?

God, You are my heavenly Father, and You love me. I feel safe with You, knowing that I am Your child and that You watch over me. Amen.

Use Your Gifts

Every good and perfect gift is from above, coming down from the Father of the heavenly lights, who does not change like shifting shadows.
JAMES 1:17 NIV

Think about all the big feelings you had this week. Were you able to let them out so they didn't become too big and overwhelming? A great way to let out those big feelings is to use the talent God gave you. Maybe you are good at singing, dancing, painting, playing a musical instrument, crafting, writing, or something else. Whatever creative gifts God has blessed you with, you can use them to express how you feel. You can dance out those big feelings, sing about them, draw them, write about them. Some of the best songs, art, and stories come from people using their talent to let out their feelings. Are you overly anxious, angry, worried, excited, joyful? Create something that shows how you feel. Don't worry about it being perfect. Just have fun using your talent to let your feelings show.

Dear God, lead me to use the creative gifts You have given me to let out my big feelings in a positive way. Amen.

Whatever creative gifts God has blessed you with, you can use them to express how you feel.

The Biggest Feeling

Do as God would do. Much-loved children want to do as their fathers do. Live with love as Christ loved you.

EPHESIANS 5:1–2 NLV

Love is the biggest feeling of all. There is a special romantic kind of love that husbands and wives feel for each other and a different feeling of love we have for family members, friends, and even our pets. The Bible talks about another kind of love that isn't only about feelings. It is about loving others even when they mess up and putting their needs ahead of our own. This kind of love is called "unconditional love." Unconditional love expects nothing in return. It is the kind of love God has for us. He loves us even when we mess up, and He forgives us. God always cares for us and provides what we need. He wants us to imitate His kind of love and to love others the way He loves us. Can you think of an example of unconditional love?

Dear Father, teach me to love others the way You love them by putting their needs ahead of my own, expecting nothing in return. Amen.

Love Is Caring and Kind

Do not work only for your own good.
Think of what you can do for others.
1 CORINTHIANS 10:24 NLV

Molly's new baby sister, Annabelle, was born with special needs. After weeks in the hospital, Annabelle came home, and with her homecoming Molly's life changed. Annabelle needed all their mother's attention, and sometimes Molly felt left out and impatient. She remembered, though, that unconditional love means putting someone's needs ahead of your own. As Molly saw her mother setting aside her own needs for Annabelle's, Molly decided to help. As she learned to care for her baby sister, Molly's love for Annabelle grew. It felt good helping her mother and sister, and as Molly helped, her mom made sure to reward Molly and make her feel appreciated and loved. It might not be easy to put someone's needs ahead of your own, but it is one of the best ways to show your love.

Lord Jesus, lead me to love others by being kind and caring, and help me to be patient when putting their needs ahead of my own. Amen.

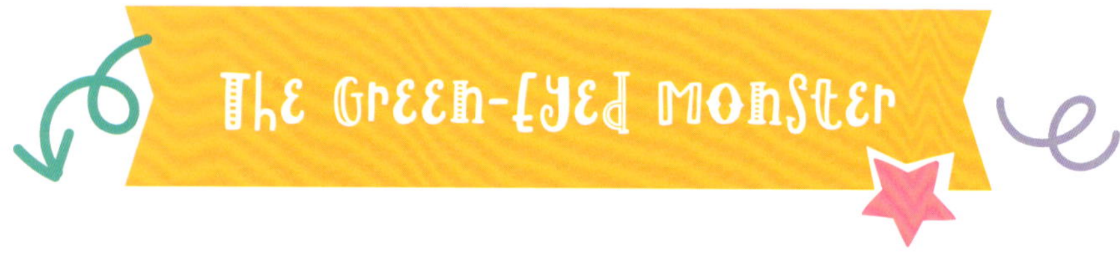

The Green-Eyed Monster

Love is not jealous.
1 CORINTHIANS 13:4 NCV

Satan hates love. In fact, he enjoys getting in the way of it. Sometimes he puts thoughts in our heads to try to lead us away from showing love and kindness to others. He tried it with Jessica. She and her best friend, Erin, were competing in the same art contest. When Erin's painting won first place, Jessica felt upset because she thought her painting was better. Jessica was jealous. We sometimes call jealousy "the green-eyed monster." (Imagine him with those green, glaring eyes, looking all angry and ugly.) Jessica knew that jealousy didn't come from God. It wasn't a loving or caring feeling. She loved Erin, and although she was disappointed, Jessica set aside her feelings and congratulated her friend for winning. Sharing in her best friend's happiness chased away the green-eyed monster. He went to hang out with Satan, where he belonged.

Dear God, I don't want anything to do with Satan and his green-eyed monster. Help me to use the love You have put in my heart to get rid of jealousy and other unkind thoughts. Amen.

Love Doesn't Brag

Love. . .does not brag.
1 CORINTHIANS 13:4 NCV

When Jessica's friend, Erin, won the art contest, she could have fallen into another of Satan's traps. Erin could have bragged about her win to Jessica. But Erin knew better. While she felt happy about winning first place, Erin understood Jessica might be unhappy that her painting hadn't won. So, rather than brag to her friend, Erin did a loving thing. She said, "Jessica, I wish you could have won first place too." Then she complimented Jessica's painting by saying how beautiful it was and what a great job Jessica had done. The Bible says love does not brag. Instead of making her own feelings most important, Erin thought about how her friend might feel, and she did her best to help Jessica feel better. It's wonderful to feel happy and proud when you win, but it's more important to think of how others might feel and to treat them with kindness and love.

Heavenly Father, thank You for reminding me to be caring and humble—to think of how others might feel and to show them some love. Amen.

Love Doesn't Get Angry

Love does not get angry. Love does not remember the suffering that comes from being hurt by someone.
1 CORINTHIANS 13:5 NLV

Hannah's youngest brother could be a pain sometimes. Tommy was four years old, and he hadn't learned that when he felt angry, he shouldn't say whatever came into his mind. One day when Hannah was babysitting Tommy, he became angry with her. "You're mean, fat, and ugly, and I hate you!" he shouted. Tommy's words hurt. But instead of getting angry, Hannah reacted quietly and with love. She allowed Tommy to calm down. Then she had a gentle talk with him about his words. Hannah hugged her brother and said, "I love you, Tommy." "I love you too," he said. Love and forgiveness healed their feelings of anger and hurt, and neither Hannah nor Tommy hung on to the mean words he had said. Everyone feels angry sometimes, and words can hurt, but it's best not to let those feelings hang around. They only become ugly and grow.

Jesus, please help me to react with love and forgiveness toward those who get angry and hurt me. Amen.

No Lie!

Love is happy with the truth.
1 CORINTHIANS 13:6 NLV

Think about this. How would you feel if you discovered someone you trusted had lied about you? Maybe you would feel angry. Anger sometimes protects our hearts from another unpleasant feeling—hurt. Lies hurt, especially when they come from a friend. The Bible says, "Telling lies about friends is like attacking them with clubs and swords and sharp arrows" (Proverbs 25:18 CEV). *Ouch!* Can you guess where lies come from? They come from Satan. He enjoys getting people to lie. "Everything he says is a lie. Not only is he a liar himself, but he is also the father of all lies" (John 8:44 CEV). God hates lies. God never lies, and He wants us not to lie too. If ever you feel like lying about someone or something, think about where lies come from. A single lie can hurt someone you love.

Dear God, I never want to hurt or disappoint You or anyone else by telling a lie. Protect me from Satan's tricks and guide me toward telling the truth. Amen.

Love Is. . .

Love is always supportive, loyal, hopeful, and trusting.
1 CORINTHIANS 13:7 CEV

Love is the biggest feeling of all because it connects to so many other good thoughts and feelings. Jesus' follower, Paul, made a list of things love is (and isn't). He wrote, "Love is patient and kind, never jealous, boastful, proud, or rude. Love isn't selfish or quick tempered. It doesn't keep a record of wrongs that others do. Love rejoices in the truth, but not in evil. Love is always supportive, loyal, hopeful, and trusting" (1 Corinthians 13:4–7 CEV). God wants to fill up your heart with His love so you can share it. As you learn to love people in many ways, God will keep filling your heart with love. Take this challenge. Spend this week finding ways to share God's love with your family, friends, and others. At the end of the week, make your own list of what you think love is.

Heavenly Father, thank You for teaching me how to love others. Fill my heart to overflowing with love so I will have plenty to share. Amen.

God is. . .

Those who do not love do not know God because God is love.
1 JOHN 4:8 NLV

Where does love come from? It comes from God. And why is love the best feeling of all? Because God *is* love! Everything He does, He does because He loves us. When He saw us falling into Satan's traps, God loved us so much that He sent Jesus to save us. There is no place in heaven for sin, the bad stuff people do. God wants all of us to live in heaven with Him forever, and Jesus made a way for that to happen. God said if we believe Jesus came to save us from sin, and if we ask Him to forgive our sin, then He will have a place ready for us in heaven when we die. There is nothing about God that isn't about love. He loves you so much that He wants to be with you and love you forever.

God, You love me! I feel it inside my heart. You watch over me, care for me, and guide me to do what is right and good. Thank You, God. Amen.

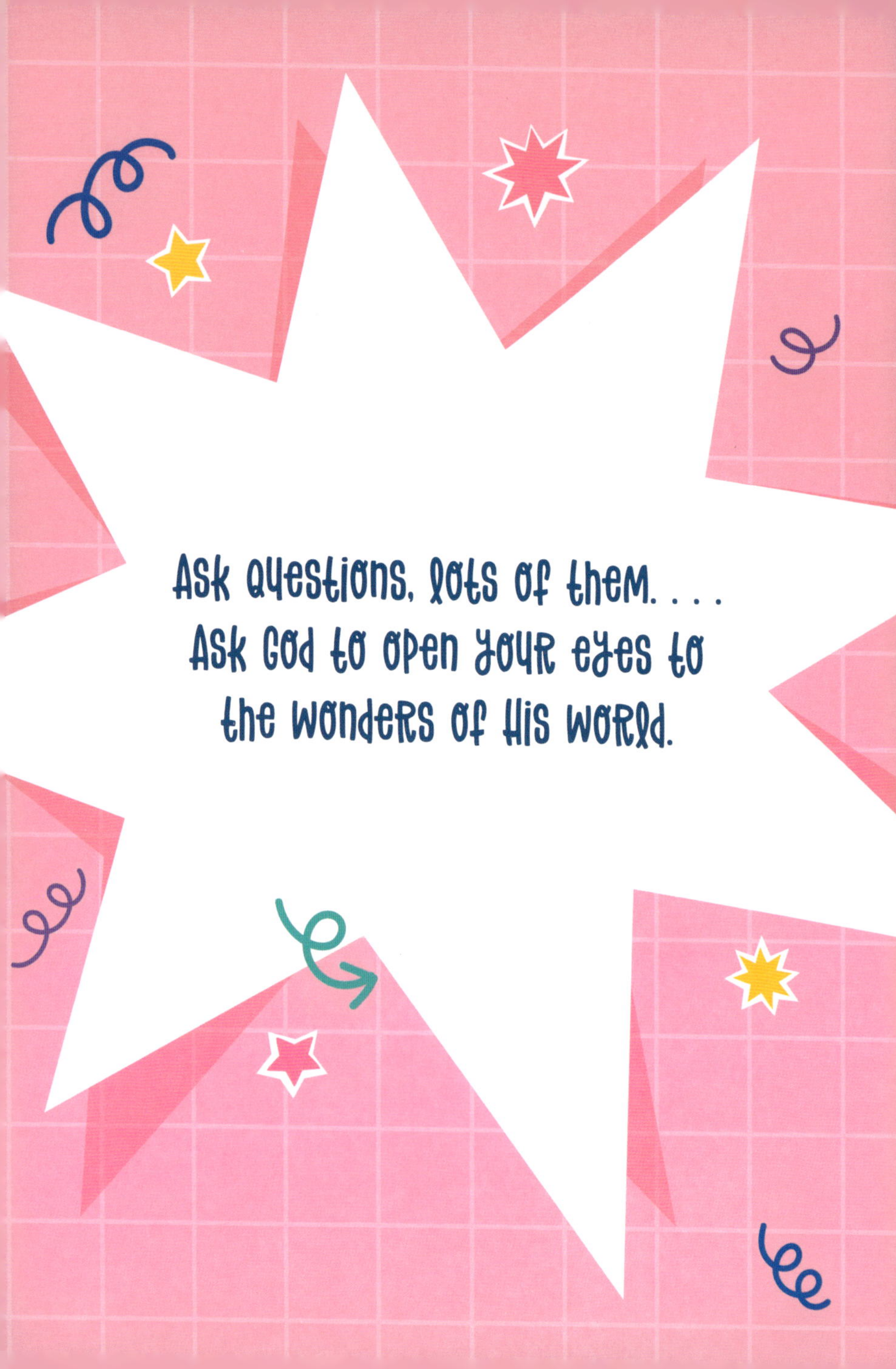
Ask questions, lots of them. . . .
Ask God to open your eyes to
the wonders of His world.

Make It Grow

Consider carefully the many wonders of God.
JOB 37:14 CEV

The next time you feel bored, cure that feeling with curiosity. Make a list of questions you wonder about. Then choose one and see if you can find the answer. Curiosity keeps our minds busy. It guides our thoughts to new ideas and possibilities. It makes us want to act on those new ideas and turn them into something real. Curiosity is exciting because it leads to travel and adventures. It makes us wonder about other countries, people, places, and cultures. It makes us curious about the earth and nature too. Most of all, curiosity is fun. Take a little feeling of curiosity and make it grow. Don't only accept someone's words about something; find your own answers. Ask questions, lots of them. See if you can find something interesting in everything, even things that bore you. Ask God to open your eyes to the wonders of His world.

Dear God, show me new things to be curious about. Grow my feelings of wonder. Teach me and help me to learn more about the world. Amen.

I Wonder About You!

In humility value others above yourselves, not looking to your own interests but each of you to the interests of the others.
PHILIPPIANS 2:3–4 NIV

In the book *The Little Prince*, the prince is curious about many things, especially when it comes to meeting new people. He enjoys learning interesting details about them, things like what games they play and whether they collect things. The Bible says we should look to the interests of others, and that's exactly what the Little Prince did. Looking to the interests of others means not only learning more about them but also helping them and caring about their needs. Asking questions and discovering what others find interesting can lead to new friendships and happiness. As you learn what they like, want, and need, a feeling of caring for others will grow inside your heart. How well do you know your friends? What do you wonder about their likes and dislikes and their families' cultures and traditions? What questions might help you to learn more about them?

Lord, please give me a feeling of wonder about people. Increase my feelings of kindness and caring for them. Amen.

I Feel Curious

God is praised for being mysterious;
rulers are praised for explaining mysteries.
PROVERBS 25:2 CEV

Mysteries were Libby's favorite kind of books. She liked putting the clues together. Libby felt curious about many things. Along with solving mysteries, she was curious about what things were, how they worked, where they came from, and why things happened. She was curious about God too—who He is, where He is, what He does, and why. Libby enjoyed learning about God by reading her Bible. It pleased God that Libby was interested in so many things. He created the world with endless mysteries for people to discover and think about. Curiosity is a feeling that leads to learning. What are you curious about? Maybe you wonder whether your dog or cat sees the way humans do. Or maybe you wonder what causes a meteor shower or why grass looks greener after a storm. When you wonder about something, don't let that feeling go. See if you can find the answers.

Heavenly Father, I'm glad that You filled the world with so many mysteries to solve. It feels good to wonder and learn new things. Amen.

I Feel Grumpy

"Do for other people whatever you would like to have them do for you."
MATTHEW 7:12 NLV

Laura woke up feeling grumpy. Rain hitting the windowpane in her bedroom made her want to roll over and go back to sleep. She didn't want to go to school. "Laura," her mom called from downstairs, "it's time to get up." Reluctantly, Laura got out of bed. Her grumpy attitude got up with her, and she really didn't care. Everyone feels like Laura sometimes. We all get grumpy, and maybe we don't want to do anything about it. It's normal to allow a little grumpiness to hang around for a bit, but it isn't good to dump it onto others. A bad attitude can hurt someone's feelings. Grumpiness can also be contagious, so don't spread it around. Whenever you feel grumpy, remember Jesus' words in Matthew 7:12. Treat others the way you would want them to treat you.

Father, some days I feel grumpy, and all I want is to be left alone. Please remind me not to allow my attitude to rub off on others. Help me to treat them with kindness and care. Amen.

A Mean Spirit

Do not be overcome by evil,
but overcome evil with good.
ROMANS 12:21 NKJV

It hurts when people are mean and say bad things about others. Being the object of someone's mean behavior can make us feel sad and even worthless or unloved. A mean attitude comes from Satan. He has another name—"the Evil One." Satan loves getting into the minds and hearts of people and leading them to hurt others. The Bible teaches us how to respond when someone is mean. It says don't be overcome by evil. In other words, we shouldn't believe that the mean things said about us are true, and we shouldn't allow someone's behavior to make us feel bad about ourselves. Satan hates anything good, so the best way to stand up to meanness is to respond as Jesus would. Do what is good and be kind. Whenever you can, turn your back to evil and walk away.

Lord Jesus, You didn't fight with mean people and say mean things back to them. You treated them with goodness and respect. Teach me to become more like You. Amen.

I like You

"I say to you who hear Me, love those who work against you. Do good to those who hate you. Respect and give thanks for those who try to bring bad to you. Pray for those who make it very hard for you."

LUKE 6:27–28 NLV

A boy in Kenzie's class was always picking on her. Kenzie felt angry and ready to say, "Back off!" but she waited. Instead, Kenzie prayed and asked Jesus what to do. She prayed for the boy too. At school the next day, Kenzie saw him sitting alone at lunch. Kenzie sat down at his table. "I don't want any trouble," she said, "but why are you mean to me? Don't you like me?" "I do like you!" he answered. Then, looking down, he said, "I guess that's why I pick on you." "I like you too," Kenzie replied, "and let's try to get along." It took courage for Kenzie to do what Jesus says in Luke 6:27–28, but it led to her and the boy becoming friends.

Jesus, when people are unkind, I will remember to obey Your words in Luke 6:27–28. Amen.

Stand Up

Open your mouth for those who cannot speak, and for the rights of those who are left without help. Open your mouth. Be right and fair in what you decide. Stand up for the rights of those who are suffering and in need.

PROVERBS 31:8–9 NLV

At the end of the school day, Sue noticed several boys in her class making fun of a younger boy. They blocked his way and stopped him from leaving the school. Sue noticed the little boy was about to cry. She wanted to help, but she didn't want to make things worse. Sue asked God to guide her. Then she went to the little boy and said, "Let's walk to the bus together." She took his arm and led him away from the bullies. Sue understood it felt scary to be bullied, and she made sure the boy got safely onto his school bus. God wants us to stand up for others, especially those who can't defend themselves. He will guide you to help on your own or lead you to ask a grown-up for help.

Dear God, lead me to help when I see others being mistreated. Amen.

I Feel Brave

Have nothing to do with the fruitless deeds of darkness, but rather expose them.
EPHESIANS 5:11 NIV

It was Heather's first year in middle school, and sometimes she felt shy and uncomfortable around the older kids. One day Heather overheard two eighth-grade boys planning to do something Heather knew was dangerous and wrong. She felt afraid to tell anyone. Heather worried what might happen to her if she told. Still, she decided to do the right thing. Heather told her mom what she heard. Her mom talked with the school's principal, and without getting Heather involved, the principal was able to stop a bad thing from happening. The Bible tells us to expose the deeds of darkness. If you hear or see someone plotting to do something bad, don't stay silent. Be brave and tell a grown-up. Also tell them if you feel worried or afraid that you might be in danger or get in trouble for telling.

Heavenly Father, if I see or hear something that could lead to trouble, help me to be brave and tell someone. My bravery might keep others from getting hurt. Amen.

EPHESIANS 5:11

Have nothing to do with the fruitless deeds of darkness, but rather expose them.

I Feel Bold

In the day when I cried out, You answered me,
and made me bold with strength in my soul.
PSALM 138:3 NKJV

Faith played basketball with her older brothers, and she played well. "I'm going to be a basketball star someday," Faith said. Her brothers laughed. "Watch me!" she told them. Faith knew it meant hard work, but she was ready. She asked God to make her strong, to give her not only a strong body but a strong spirit to keep her from becoming discouraged or afraid. First, she played basketball on a junior team. Then, in high school Faith led her girls' team to win the state championship. Several colleges wanted Faith to play on their teams. She became a star college basketball player who went on to play in the Olympics. Faith had a bold spirit—she was not afraid of hard work and difficult or risky situations. Can you remember a time when you felt bold, fearless, and ready to take a risk?

Lord, give me a bold spirit. Make me unafraid of doing what is hard, and give me strength to work toward my goals. Amen.

Solomon's Wisdom

Please make me wise and teach me the difference between right and wrong.
1 KINGS 3:9 CEV

Solomon became king of Israel when he was young, probably around the age of today's high school kids. Solomon didn't know how to rule a kingdom, and he likely felt nervous and afraid. The Bible says Solomon prayed and asked God to make him wise and teach him the difference between right and wrong. God said yes to Solomon's prayer. King Solomon ruled Israel for forty years, and as he got older, he grew in wisdom. He became known as the wisest man who ever lived. Many of Solomon's wise sayings appear in the Bible in the book of Proverbs. If you feel uneasy about taking on a big responsibility, think about Solomon and his prayer. Ask God to give you wisdom, not only to do the job but to be fair and do it the right way.

Dear God, whenever I face a new responsibility, if I feel worried or nervous, please bless me with wisdom. Show me what to do and teach me the right way to do it. Amen.

That Was Foolish!

Go away from a foolish man, for you will not find words of much learning.
PROVERBS 14:7 NLV

Can people fly like a bird or a superhero? Of course they can't. At a family picnic in the park, Holly's younger cousins were swinging on the swings and pretending to be superheroes. "Watch me fly!" one of them shouted. He jumped off his swing high in the air, fell, and broke his wrist. Jumping off the swing was a foolish idea. Solomon said to stay away from foolish ideas. Foolishness is doing what you know is unwise. Foolishness usually fails, and it can end with people getting hurt. Foolishness can lead to feeling embarrassed too, especially when others see us not using common sense. Solomon says in Proverbs 14:7 there isn't much learning in foolishness. Can you think of something foolish you did that failed? Describe your feelings when it didn't end well. Did you learn not to do it again? God wants us to be wise about everything we say and do.

Father God, keep me away from foolish ideas. Please lead me toward wisdom and using good sense. Amen.

I Feel Silly

"The city will be filled with boys and girls playing."
ZECHARIAH 8:5 NLV

Silliness can lead to good and happy feelings. Maybe you and your girlfriends sing along to favorite songs and change the lyrics to make them silly. Maybe you have fun wearing silly costumes, playing silly games, or just laughing and being silly together. Silliness is different from foolishness. Silly doesn't mean doing what is unwise. Instead, it is about acting goofy, giggling, and having fun. Silliness is a joyful feeling. God wants us to be happy, and silly is okay with Him if it is good fun that He would approve of. It isn't okay when silliness makes fun of others or imitates something God wouldn't like. Enjoy yourself. Be silly. God is watching, and He loves seeing his children playing and feeling happy.

Heavenly Father, I'm glad that silliness is okay with You. My friends and I get silly sometimes when we are together. We laugh a lot. I will make sure that our silliness is always good, clean fun that would make You smile. Amen.

I Feel Frustrated

"The Lord will fight for you.
All you have to do is keep still."
EXODUS 14:14 NLV

Nora had done her best to learn about dividing fractions, but she just didn't get it. She hated math. One afternoon while doing homework, Nora said, "This is *so* frustrating!" Then she started to cry. Frustration is another of those crazy, mixed-up feelings. It happens when you can't accomplish what you want or get what you want. When frustration shows up, it leads to feeling irritated, annoyed, discouraged, or angry. It can make you feel like giving up. It can even make you cry. Hot tears rolled down Nora's face as she remembered a Bible verse: "The Lord will fight for you. All you have to do is keep still." Before trying the math problem again, Nora talked with God. Then, when she still couldn't work the problem, God led her to talk with her mom. They planned for Nora to get the help she needed so math wouldn't seem so hard.

Dear God, I will be still. Please speak to me. Calm my frustration and show me what to do. Amen.

I Feel Discouraged

"This is what the LORD says to you: 'Do not be afraid or discouraged because of this vast army. For the battle is not yours, but God's.' "
2 CHRONICLES 20:15 NIV

Discouraged is the feeling you get when you've tried your best to accomplish something but failed. Sometimes discouragement can make you feel like the whole world is against you. Satan loves trapping us in feelings of discouragement. But God is way more powerful and much smarter than Satan! When discouragement attacks and steals your good feelings, God will fight for you. Trust in that promise. Set your thoughts on Him and everything good. And remember that God always wins His battles. You can help to fight discouragement by reminding yourself that you are courageous, strong, capable, and an awesome child of God. Can you remember a time when you felt discouraged? What made you feel better?

God, I feel like I can't do anything right. Please fight this battle for me. I'm thinking right now about how much You love me, and I know You will help and encourage me. Amen.

PROVERBS 10:19

If you talk a lot,
you are sure to sin;
if you are wise,
you will keep quiet.

Shhh. . .

If you talk a lot, you are sure to sin;
if you are wise, you will keep quiet.
PROVERBS 10:19 NCV

If you've heard people argue, maybe you noticed them talking at each other and neither listening to what the other was saying. They talked and talked and became more and more frustrated and angry. The Bible says, "If you are wise, you will keep quiet." When people are upset with each other, listening is important because it can stop an argument from becoming worse. Listening to a person's words and trying to understand their feelings is what Jesus wants us to do. If you begin arguing with someone, stop. Listen, be understanding, and then do one more thing—put to work what you've learned from the Bible. Apologize if you've done something wrong. Use gentle words. And if you can't calm angry feelings, then take a break and rest for a while with Jesus. Ask Him to lead you and show you what to do.

Lord Jesus, help me to listen instead of arguing. Guide me to use what You've taught me about being kind and getting along. Amen.

A Gentle Answer

A gentle answer turns away anger,
but a sharp word causes anger.
PROVERBS 15:1 NLV

Charlotte's older sister, Kate, rushed into their bedroom. "Did you take my sweater?" she shouted. "I've told you a thousand times to ask before you borrow my stuff!" Kate continued her angry words while Charlotte sat on her bed silently listening. Charlotte had learned from the Bible that arguing with her sister was a foolish idea. Instead, she decided to try what Solomon said in Proverbs 15:1. "You're right," she said gently. "I should have asked first, and I'm sorry. Can you forgive me?" Kate was surprised by Charlotte's response; she had expected a fight. Kate's anger began to melt away. "I'm sorry I yelled at you," she said. "And I forgive you." Solomon's wise words had told Charlotte what to do, and her gentle response helped to calm her sister's anger. God is pleased when He sees His children use what they've learned from the Bible, especially if it helps them to get along.

Heavenly Father, I'm learning a lot about feelings by reading Your Word, and I'm doing my best to use what I've learned. Amen.

A Cheerful Heart

The cheerful heart has a continual feast.
PROVERBS 15:15 NIV

Melissa dreamed a silly dream. She was dressed like a queen and seated on a throne inside an old castle. In front of her was a long table set with an amazing feast. Every kind of food Melissa loved was there: every kind of pie and cake, cookies, candy, pizza, ice cream, soda. . . Looking at that lovely feast, smelling it, and tasting it made Queen Melissa happy. It was a good dream, and when she woke up, Melissa felt cheerful. The Bible says, "The cheerful heart has a continual feast." Each day, God puts good things in front of us, things we like and love. Can you name a few? When you think about all those good things, then cheerfulness will grow inside your heart. As in Melissa's dream, you will see before you all kinds of wonderful things—a feast for all your senses.

Lord, help me to notice all the good things You put around me. Give me a cheerful heart, a heart that appreciates and finds joy in all Your creations. Amen.

I Know You Can!

Whoever has the gift of encouraging others should encourage.

ROMANS 12:8 NCV

Jenny saw that her friend Stacy was busy creating something. "What are you making?" Jenny asked. Stacy answered, "I feel so discouraged. I'm trying to make a bracelet for my mom, but whatever I do, I just can't get it right. I'm ready to give up." Jenny had learned from the Bible to care about how others feel and to be an encourager. "You're great at making jewelry!" she said. "Keep trying. I know you can do it." Jenny watched as Stacy worked. "That looks nice," she said. "You're so talented." Jenny's words encouraged her friend not to give up and to feel more confident about her work. Just as with Jenny, God has put inside your heart the gift to be an encourager, but it's up to you to use His gift. Your encouraging words might be just what someone needs to boost their confidence and to keep going.

Lord, You have placed the gift of encouragement inside my heart. Teach me to use it to help others feel good about themselves. Amen.

A Little Help, Please

Iron is made sharp with iron,
and one man is made sharp by a friend.
PROVERBS 27:17 NLV

Maybe you've watched your mom or dad sharpen kitchen knives so they cut better. Knives need help to stay sharp. People need help to stay sharp too. Solomon said, "One man is made sharp by a friend." He meant that friends can help us to become even better than we are right now. Ecclesiastes 4:9–10 (NLV) says, "Two are better than one, because. . .if one of them falls, the other can help him up." Have you ever felt helpless? You don't have to feel embarrassed or ashamed to ask for help. Everyone needs help sometimes to learn new things, to get out of trouble, or to do something they can't do alone. It's perfectly okay to say, "A little help, please," and to accept help from others. And don't forget to ask God for help too. He is the best helper of all.

Dear God, when I need help, thank You for being my helper and for leading me to others who will help. Amen.

I Feel Embarrassed

"Don't be embarrassed, because you will not be disgraced. You will forget the shame you felt earlier."
ISAIAH 54:4 NCV

Mindy was chosen to play the lead in the school play. She had tons of lines to memorize, and she worked hard to get them right. Everything went well in the rehearsals, but on the first night of the play, when she walked on stage and saw a huge audience, Mindy froze in fear. She couldn't remember her lines. After standing there for what seemed like forever, Mindy's costar whispered the lines to her. Mindy felt embarrassed when everyone saw her mess up. It happens to everyone—fear and other emotions can cause mess-ups. It's nothing to be ashamed of. God gave Mindy courage to perform well in the rest of the play. At the end, when the audience clapped for her and cheered, Mindy forgot the embarrassment she had felt. She forgave herself for messing up. She knew she would do better next time.

Father in heaven, I feel embarrassed when people see my mistakes. Help me to remember that innocent mess-ups are nothing to be ashamed of. Amen.

I Feel Ashamed

If we tell Him our sins, He is faithful and we can depend on Him to forgive us of our sins. He will make our lives clean from all sin.

1 JOHN 1:9 NLV

There is a difference between innocent mistakes like forgetting lines in a play and mess-ups caused by sin. For example, if your dad said, "No screen time after supper," and you got caught watching videos, your mess-up was caused by sin. You did something you knew was wrong. Shame is a feeling connected with sinful mess-ups. We feel ashamed for doing what we know God and others disapprove of. The way we get rid of our shame is to tell God what we did and ask Him to forgive us. No matter how often we sin, God will forgive us when we ask. We don't have to carry our shame around like a heavy sack of potatoes. When God forgives us, He gives us a fresh start.

I'm sorry, God. What I did was wrong, and I knew it. Please forgive me. I will try harder to do what is good and right. Amen.

Jesus Understands

Jesus understands every weakness of ours, because he was tempted in every way that we are. But he did not sin!
HEBREWS 4:15 CEV

When Jesus lived here on earth, He had feelings like ours. Jesus felt happy, sad, loving, kind, caring, disappointed, irritated, and even angry. The difference between us and Jesus is that His feelings never led Him to sin. When Satan tried to get Him to sin, Jesus had control of His emotions. He never gave in. We aren't perfect like Jesus, so sometimes our emotions get out of control and we fall for Satan's tricks. When that happens, it's important to remember that Jesus understands us. Although He never sinned, Jesus saw plenty of sin while He was here, and He felt our sins when He died for us on the cross. Whatever you are feeling, remember that Jesus understands. Talk with Him about your feelings, good and bad. Know that He loves you, forgives you, and will help you to do better.

Lord Jesus, I'm glad You are my friend. I feel comfortable telling You about my feelings because I know You understand me. Amen.

When Someone Dies

Jesus said to her, "I am the One Who raises the dead and gives them life. Anyone who puts his trust in Me will live again, even if he dies."

JOHN 11:25 NLV

Keisha sat on her bed sobbing. Her mom held her tight. Keisha's grandma had just died, and Kiesha had a deep ache inside, a big feeling she hadn't felt before. "Let's pray and ask Jesus to comfort us," said Keisha's mom. "Grandma is with Jesus right now, and she's happy and well." Kiesha and her mom remembered Jesus' promise that everyone who believes in Him will live in heaven after they die. Keisha still felt sad because she would miss her grandma. But she felt a little better knowing that Grandma was in heaven and she would see her again someday. When we die, we leave our bodies behind, but if we believe in Jesus, we get new and perfect bodies in heaven. In heaven there is no sadness. It's okay to hurt when someone dies. Jesus promises to comfort us, and in time we will feel better.

Jesus, I feel so sad. Please comfort me and wipe away my tears. Amen.

Compassion

"The LORD, the LORD, the compassionate and gracious God, slow to anger, abounding in love and faithfulness."
EXODUS 34:6 NIV

Compassion is the feeling we get when we notice people suffering and we want to help. When we think of Jesus, we think of compassion. God's Son came to earth to help people, to teach them to live right, and to lead them to forever life in heaven. When sick people came to Him, Jesus had compassion on them. He made them well. He cast demons out of them, He made the deaf hear, the blind see, and the lame walk. Wherever He went, Jesus showed compassion—faithfulness, kindness, and love. Compassion is a feeling that wants to grow inside our hearts. Do you know someone who needs help? How about people in your community, your church, and the world? Think of ways to show them compassion. What could you do to help ease their suffering?

Lord, You are the best example of compassion. Help me to grow compassion inside my heart. Show me how to help those who are suffering and in need. Amen.

EXODUS 34:6

"The LORD, the LORD, the compassionate and gracious God, slow to anger, abounding in love and faithfulness."

I Feel Compassionate

All of you, be like-minded, be sympathetic, love one another, be compassionate and humble.
1 PETER 3:8 NIV

Julie made a list of people who needed some help. Her great-grandma couldn't do yard work anymore. She needed help with that. A boy in her school was sick in the hospital. He needed to know that his friends cared about him. People in her community were hungry. They needed food. As her list grew, Julie jotted down ways to help. She and her brother could volunteer to care for their great-grandma's yard. She could ask her teacher about the class making cards to send to her classmate in the hospital. Julie and her mom could shop for food to donate to their community's food bank. The more ways she found to help, the more Julie's compassion grew. And as it grew, Julie felt closer to Jesus. She was His helper, doing His work here on earth.

Dear Jesus, I want to help others, but I don't always know what to do. Please give me some ideas. Make me Your helper, Your servant here on earth. Amen.

I Feel Helpful

"If anyone wants to serve Me, he must follow Me. So where I am, the one who wants to serve Me will be there also. If anyone serves Me, My Father will honor him."
JOHN 12:26 NLV

We learn how to help others by following Jesus' example. When people needed help, Jesus never turned them away. Many learned from Him to be kind, gentle, and more loving. Today we learn about Jesus by reading the first four books in the Bible's New Testament: Matthew, Mark, Luke, and John. When we follow Jesus' example of helping others, God fills our hearts with even more caring, compassion, and love to give away. Learn all you can about Jesus. Do your best to help others in ways that would please Him. Even if you receive nothing in return, not even a thank-you, remember that the good feelings connected with helpfulness come from the Lord. Keep on being helpful and make those feelings grow.

Lord Jesus, I want to learn as much as I can about You. I want to serve You here on earth by treating everyone with gentle loving-kindness. Amen.

No Thanks

Do not be quick to say who is right or wrong. Wait until the Lord comes. . . . He will show why men have done these things. Every man will receive from God the thanks he should have.

1 CORINTHIANS 4:5 NLV

Claire did her best to be helpful like Jesus. Being helpful felt good until one day it didn't. Claire knew a girl whose family was poor. She came to school dressed in shabby clothes. After asking her mom's permission, Claire planned to give the girl shirts and sweaters she didn't wear anymore. But when she tried to give them away, the girl got angry and said, "I don't need your old stuff!" Claire didn't expect that reaction. She thought the girl would thank her. Claire told her mom, "She was wrong not to thank me! That's what I get for trying to help." Her mom answered, "But God saw, and *He* said thank you." Claire had forgotten that we show kindness not to please others and ourselves, but only to please God.

Dear God, knowing You are happy when I am helpful and kind is all the thanks I need. Amen.

"Follow Me"

Jesus said to His followers, "If anyone wants to be My follower, he must forget about himself. He must take up his cross and follow Me."
MATTHEW 16:24 NLV

When Ella read Matthew 16:24, she wondered what it meant to take up one's cross. She asked her pastor. He said it means doing what Jesus would do even when people make fun of you and hurt your feelings for following Him. It means being like Jesus by putting the needs of others before your own. Ella understood that following Jesus wouldn't always feel good. People might make fun of her; others could try to turn her away from Jesus by tempting her to sin. Sometimes Jesus would ask her to do something new or something difficult that made her feel a little scared. Still, Ella was ready to be totally committed to Jesus because she knew it would lead her someplace good.

Jesus, when You carried Your cross, people made fun of You. Still, You gave Your life so I could have forever life in heaven. Help me to be more like You and put the needs of others before my own. Amen.

Did Jesus Ever. . .?

Then Jesus went into the house of God and made all those leave who were buying and selling there. He turned over the tables of the men who changed money. He turned over the seats of those who sold doves.

MATTHEW 21:12 NLV

Ella wondered if Jesus ever felt angry. When she read Matthew 21:12, she discovered that Jesus felt angry with merchants selling their goods in God's temple. Jesus also felt irritated by proud religious leaders who wouldn't believe He was God's Son. He felt irritated with His disciples when they tried to keep little children from coming to Him. Jesus wanted people to love and obey God and to feel welcomed by Him. Jesus' anger came from His feelings of hurt when people chose to sin. Although Jesus sometimes felt angry, He never held on to those angry feelings. Instead, Jesus showed mercy. He prayed for people, and He did His best to teach them what is right and good.

Dear Jesus, You calmed Your anger by praying for others and showing them mercy. Please teach me to be more like You when anger comes into my heart. Amen.

I Feel Merciful

*"Blessed are the merciful,
for they will be shown mercy."*
MATTHEW 5:7 NIV

Mercy is when we show forgiveness and kindness to people who don't deserve it. When Claire tried giving some of her shirts and sweaters to a girl in need and the girl felt angry instead of thankful, Claire learned about mercy. When Claire and her mom talked about it, Claire decided the girl had reacted that way because she felt embarrassed. She didn't want others to know she needed new clothes. Although Claire had been treated unkindly, she felt merciful toward the girl. Claire forgave her and continued to be friendly and kind. God treats us with mercy all the time. Whenever we do things that don't please Him, He is quick to forgive us, and He never stops loving us or treating us with kindness. God is pleased when we feel mercy for others. It's good to know that we share that feeling with God.

Dear God, I mess up sometimes, and I don't deserve Your mercy, but it is there for me all the time. Thank You for being merciful to me. Amen.

When It's Hard to Forgive

But even in judgment, God is merciful!
JAMES 2:13 CEV

Sometimes forgiveness feels impossible. Cassie's brother died in a car crash. Cassie felt *so* angry. The other driver was sorry for causing the accident, but still Cassie wanted him punished in the worst possible way. One night Cassie heard her parents praying aloud. "Dear Lord," her dad said, "our sadness feels overwhelming, but we know our son is safe with You." "Please forgive the young man who caused the accident," Cassie's mom continued. "We pray that You will show him mercy and that the court will punish him fairly." Her dad ended the prayer, "It's not for us to judge, Lord. It's up to You." After listening to their prayer, Cassie prayed silently, asking God to comfort her. Then, even though the words were hard to say, Cassie asked God to be merciful when He judged the other driver. When we leave it with God to judge others, He begins to take away some of our anger and pain.

Father God, comfort my sadness and calm my anger. I leave it to You to judge those who hurt me. Amen.

Really Big Feelings

*Try to understand other people. Forgive each other.
If you have something against someone,
forgive him. That is the way the Lord forgave you.*
COLOSSIANS 3:13 NLV

Anger and sadness are really *big* feelings. They stick with us, and it's hard to get rid of them. Often, to make them go away, we must offer forgiveness. Forgiveness is hard work. It doesn't mean we think what caused our sadness or anger is okay. Instead, forgiveness is accepting what happened and then giving the rest to God—leaving the situation in His hands. We might have to do that over and over again until we begin to feel less angry. God knows what to do. He knows whether and how to punish those who hurt us. He wants us to let go of our hurt and anger and feel happy again. If you feel anger hanging around inside you, ask God for help getting rid of it. Then trust Him to make it happen.

God, what someone did hurt me badly. Forgiving is hard. Please help me to let go of the anger inside me. I want to feel happy again. Amen.

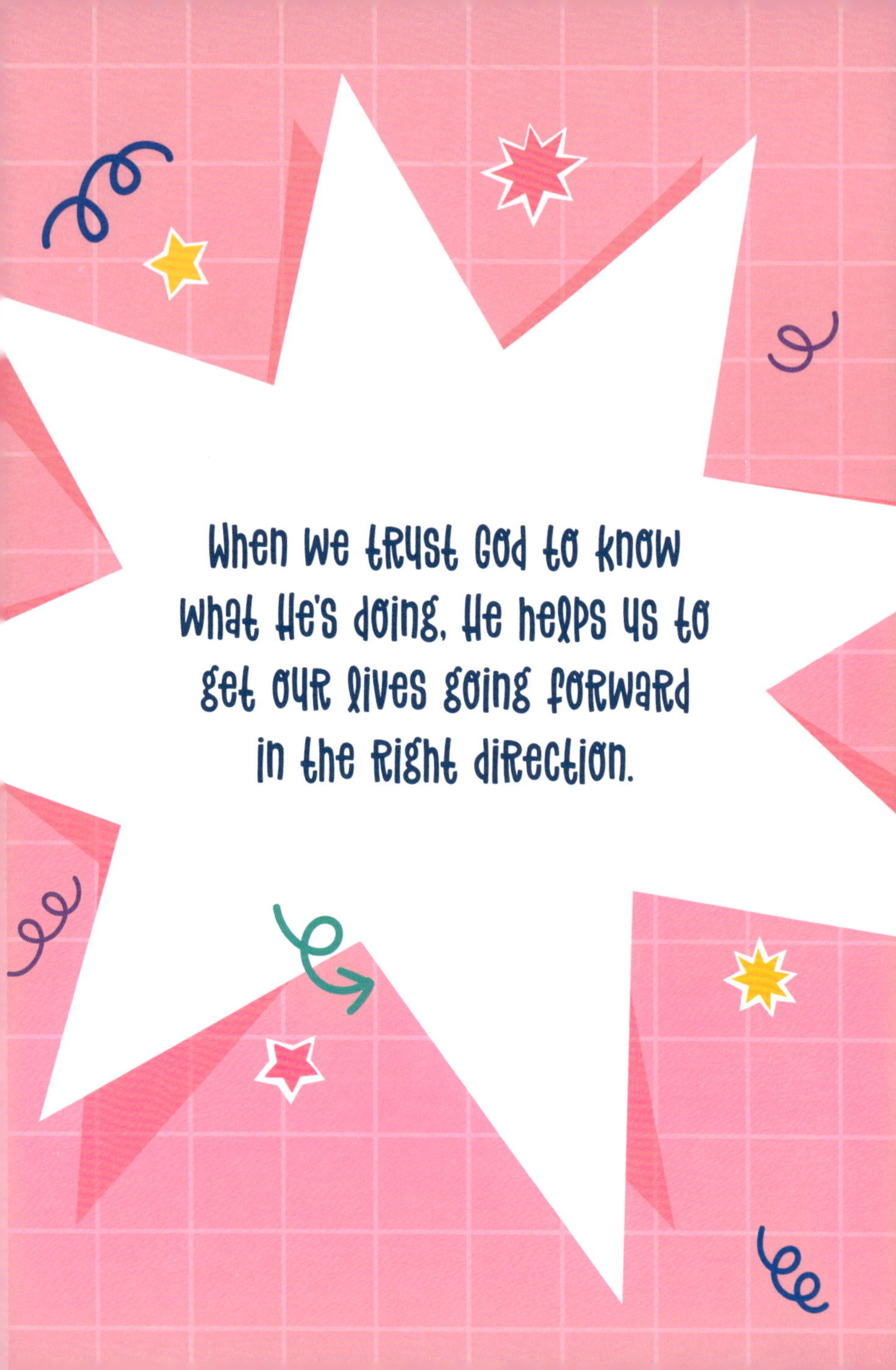
When we trust God to know
what He's doing, He helps us to
get our lives going forward
in the right direction.

Why?

Trust in the Lord with all your heart, and do not trust in your own understanding. Agree with Him in all your ways, and He will make your paths straight.

PROVERBS 3:5–6 NLV

As Cassie tried to forgive the man whose careless driving had killed her brother, she asked God many questions. "Why did this happen? Why didn't You stop it? Why *my* brother?" Cassie felt frustrated when there were no answers. She didn't understand why this terrible thing had happened. Some things we will never understand until we meet God in heaven and can ask Him. In the meantime, the Bible tells us to keep trusting God, especially when we can't understand. Cassie's frustration finally went away when she could accept that God loved her brother and had His reasons for wanting her brother in heaven. Still, she hurt. She would miss her brother always, but it helped knowing he was safe and happy with God. When we trust God to know what He's doing, He helps us to get our lives going forward in the right direction.

Heavenly Father, I don't understand Your ways, but I trust You to do what is right. Amen.

I Feel Present

"Do not worry about tomorrow. Tomorrow will have its own worries."
MATTHEW 6:34 NLV

"I feel present." That sounds strange, doesn't it? Feeling present happens when you are concentrating on what's going on in this very moment instead of dwelling on what happened in the past or could happen in the future. Jesus said we shouldn't worry about tomorrow. Nobody knows for sure what will happen tomorrow or even later today. When we trust Jesus with the future and remember that He is here with us right now—in the present—then we feel less worried and afraid. Right now you are reading this book. Are you thinking about these words, or is your mind somewhere else? When you practice being present, in this very moment, you will learn to stay focused. That's a skill you want to learn because it will help you at school and all through your life.

Dear Jesus, my mind wanders a lot, and I feel worried about stuff that might happen. I know I don't have to worry because I can trust You to lead me through every minute. Help me, Lord, to be present. Amen.

Here I Am

"Then you will call, and the Lord will answer. You will cry, and He will say, 'Here I am.'"
ISAIAH 58:9 NLV

Sadie's dad was in the military and their family moved a lot. Sadie was used to moving, but still she felt nervous about starting at a new school. Often when Sadie's family moved, the school year had already begun. Sadie hated being the new kid. She lay awake the night before her first day thinking about everything that might happen. Suddenly she heard the words "Here I am" pop into her thoughts. It made her remember that Jesus was right there with her. She remembered too that Jesus had said not to worry about tomorrow. Sadie felt comforted and at peace knowing that Jesus was with her in that very moment and that He would be with her in each minute of the next day. When you feel nervous, worried, or afraid, call for Jesus. He will answer, "Here I am."

Lord Jesus, thank You for being with me right now when I feel worried and afraid. I will give all my worries to You and trust You to guide me. Amen.

I Feel Peaceful and Calm

But I am calm and quiet, like a baby with its mother.
I am at peace, like a baby with its mother.
PSALM 131:2 NCV

Sadie was surprised by how calm she felt on her first day in a new school. She kept thinking about Jesus saying to her, "Here I am." When Sadie thought of Him, she felt peaceful. Can you remember a time when you rested in your parents' arms and felt peaceful and safe? Jesus wants you to feel like you are resting in His big, strong arms all night and all day. If you can imagine Jesus walking by your side, holding your hand and keeping you safe, it will help get you through all those scary firsts—the first day of school, the first time away from home without your parents, the first heartbreak. . . Whatever new thing you face, Jesus will guide you through it and help you feel peaceful and calm.

Jesus, I can feel You with me right now. I feel Your presence whenever I remember that You are always with me, helping me and keeping me safe and sound. Amen.

I Feel Serene

The Lord is my Shepherd. I will have everything I need. He lets me rest in fields of green grass. He leads me beside the quiet waters.
PSALM 23:1–2 NLV

Serene is a word that describes feeling peaceful and calm. God puts all kinds of beautiful things in the world to help us feel serene. Some people find that petting a dog or cat helps them to feel serene. Others feel calm and peaceful floating in their swimming pool on a warm, sunny day, walking in the woods, resting in a field of green grass, or being near a calm lake or quiet stream. Everything that gives us serene feelings comes from God. Isn't that wonderful? God loves us so much that He creates things, places, people, and situations to help us feel peaceful, calm, and safe. Think about it: What makes you feel serene? As you think of each thing, give thanks to God.

Dear God, I feel serene just thinking of all the peaceful and cozy things You have put in the world for me to enjoy. Thank You for every one of them. Amen.

I Feel Cozy

Your love has given me much joy and comfort.
PHILEMON 7 NLV

In Denmark it is a custom to enjoy *hygge*. The word is pronounced "hoo-gah," and it describes a setting where we feel cozy, comfortable, and content. Winter is the most hygge season of all. It is very hygge, for example, to drink cocoa by the fireplace. Dinner by candlelight is hygge. Snuggling under a warm blanket while listening to soft music or reading a good book is hygge too. Hygge is anywhere or anything at all that makes you feel calm, cozy, and relaxed, either by yourself or with others. Imagine a hygge setting at Christmastime. Where is someplace cozy you would like to be? What things would make you feel cozy? A quiet kind of joyfulness comes with hygge. It comes when God's love fills our hearts with good and cozy feelings. Not only in winter but all year long, find time for coziness. Imagine God's love creating a warm glow inside your heart.

Heavenly Father, I feel even nearer to You when I am someplace cozy where I am peaceful, calm, and content. Amen.

Love Each Other

[Jesus said,] "I give you a new Law. You are to love each other. You must love each other as I have loved you."
JOHN 13:34 NLV

Trisha's youngest brother, Randy, felt upset whenever he heard loud noises and when things at home seemed out of order or new. Calming him was difficult. Trisha began noticing times when Randy felt calm. She paid attention to where he was, what he was doing, and the things that made him feel cozy and comfortable. Trisha learned to create a cozy setting for Randy when he felt upset. She made him feel loved as she sat with him and snuggled him. Helping someone to feel comfortable is one way we show them love. Trisha's family joined her in bringing comfort to Randy and to others. They volunteered by serving hot meals to the hungry, donated warm clothes to those who were cold, and welcomed new members to their church. They did their best to love others the way Jesus would love them.

Dear Jesus, teach me to love others by helping them to feel comfortable, cozy, and calm. Amen.

I Can't Sleep

I will lie down and sleep in peace.
O Lord, You alone keep me safe.
PSALM 4:8 NLV

Nia's dance team had earned a place in a national competition. In addition to the group dance, Nia was dancing a solo. The night before the competition, Nia felt more nervous than ever. She could feel her heart pounding as she lay in bed. The dark, unfamiliar hotel room added to her anxiety. She felt grateful that her mom was with her. Nia tried to sleep. It was important to get her rest. But all Nia could do was worry. It might help if she remembered Psalm 4:8. King David wrote it when he felt anxious. He knew he could sleep in peace because God had all his worries under control. Do you ever have trouble sleeping? Try talking with God. Trust Him with your troubles. He will guide you and keep you safe.

Dear God, I can't sleep! So much is going on, and my thoughts are all over the place. I feel safe and comfortable when I'm near You. Let's talk awhile. Then please help me to sleep in peace. Amen.

So Many Moods

Why am I discouraged? Why am I restless? I trust you, LORD! And I will praise you again because you help me, and you are my God.
PSALM 42:11 CEV

Brooke came home from school in a bad mood. "What's going on with you?" asked her mom. "Nothing," Brooke said. It was the best answer she could come up with. She didn't know what was going on with her; she just felt moody. Her feelings were all over the place for no good reason. One minute everything seemed fine. Then she felt like crying. She felt restless and discouraged and irritated too. Maybe you have felt like Brooke. All girls have days when their emotions get tangled. It's normal. The good news is that it doesn't last. If you trust in the Lord to help you untangle those moods, He will. When you feel moody, try thinking of everything that's good, and spend a little quiet time with God.

Father in heaven, I don't know why I'm so moody. I just am! I know You will straighten out my feelings. I'm starting to feel better already. Thank You, God. Amen.

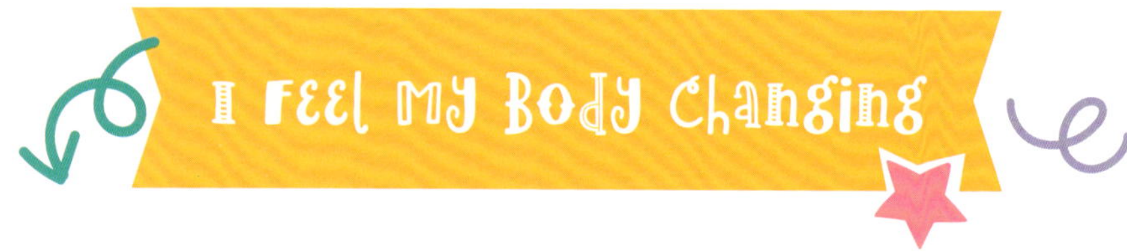

I Feel My Body Changing

God wants each of you to use his body in the right way by keeping it holy and by respecting it.
1 THESSALONIANS 4:4 NLV

All kids your age go through a time when their bodies begin to change. Some kids feel uncomfortable with those changes. They might even be unsure how they feel inside their "new" more grown-up bodies. Peer pressure can make things even more confusing. It helps to remember that God created our bodies. He made the cells that make up all our parts. He made you a girl by giving you different chromosomes than boys. Inside your chromosomes are genes that determined your skin, eye, and hair color and many other things. God makes each of us exactly the way He wants us to be. It can be a bit uncomfortable getting used to a changing body, but remember that most changes take time before they feel comfortable. God wants us to respect our bodies and honor Him for making each of us special and unique.

Dear God, as my body changes, guide me to use it in ways that respect and honor You. Amen.

God wants each of you to use his body in the right way by keeping it holy and by respecting it.

A Happy Heart

I praise you because you made me in an amazing and wonderful way. What you have done is wonderful. I know this very well.
PSALM 139:14 NCV

How do you feel about yourself? Do you feel good about yourself just as you are? It's even better if you love yourself. You should love yourself! Why? Because God made you in an amazing and wonderful way. Everything God makes is wonderful and beautiful in its own way. Beauty isn't only about what we see on the outside. In fact, the most beautiful part of every human being is the heart. Not the organ God created that keeps us alive, but the "heart" that is an invisible place deep inside us where all our feelings are stored. God doesn't want you to have a heart that feels miserable. He wants you to have a happy heart because a happy heart makes you feel good about yourself and others. Think about it: How does your heart feel today?

Heavenly Father, give me a happy heart, a heart that is grateful to You for loving me and making me Your amazing and wonderful child. Amen.

Maybe I Can Help

We were sent to speak for Christ, and God is begging you to listen to our message.
2 CORINTHIANS 5:20 CEV

You are getting better at understanding your own feelings and becoming more aware of how others might feel. Now you can use what you've learned to help. If you have siblings, notice how they handle feelings like anger, sadness, fear, and disappointment. Share with them what you've learned to get rid of those ugly feelings. At school you can set a good example by how you react when something makes you feel hurt, angry, or disappointed. You can teach others about compassion and kindness by the way you treat people who feel sad or need help. You are like one of Jesus' disciples helping people here on earth. Remember to share with them what you know about Jesus and how He behaved.

Dear Jesus, I'm learning from You how to handle my feelings. I'm getting better at letting go of those that are ugly and I'm growing those that are good. I want to show my family and friends how to do that too. Amen.

Make Them Grow

"It is like a mustard seed which a man took and planted in his field. It grew and became a tree. The birds of the sky stayed in its branches."
LUKE 13:19 NLV

When God made us, He put only good feelings inside our hearts. We can think of Him like a gardener planting seeds. Inside our hearts, God put seeds of caring, compassion, love, generosity, kindness, joy, forgiveness. . . We were born with those good feelings, but God expects us to make them grow. Growing good feelings takes some work and attention. It's important to keep ugly feelings from sneaking in like weeds. Selfishness, jealousy, anger, depression, impatience, and loneliness are just some of the ugly feelings we don't want to grow. We need to recognize them right away and then get rid of them. Praying, talking about our feelings, and thinking good thoughts help to grow good feelings. Can you think of other ways to make good feelings grow?

Dear God, please show me how to keep ugly feelings from entering my heart. I want my good feelings to grow big and strong like a tree with branches that touch the sky. Amen.

The Holy Spirit

But the fruit that comes from having the Holy Spirit in our lives is: love, joy, peace, not giving up, being kind, being good, having faith, being gentle, and being the boss over our own desires.
GALATIANS 5:22–23 NLV

When we ask Jesus to come into our hearts, He gives us another part of Himself, a part called the Holy Spirit. The Holy Spirit is our helper. He guides us to live in ways that please God. He is that feeling inside our hearts that says, "Watch out," or "That's not right." The Holy Spirit helps us to grow our good feelings and become more loving, happy, peaceful, patient, kind, good, faithful, gentle, and self-controlled. If you have asked Jesus to live inside your heart, then you can be sure the Holy Spirit lives there too. God, Jesus, and the Holy Spirit all work together to help your good feelings grow.

Lord God, what an amazing Father You are. You rule the universe; You gave us Your Son, Jesus, to lead us to all things good; You gave us another helper, the Holy Spirit, to guide our feelings. Thank You, God! Amen.

Listen and Obey

[Jesus said,] "The Helper is the Holy Spirit. The Father will send Him in My place. He will teach you everything and help you remember everything I have told you."
JOHN 14:26 NLV

Gianna was at a friend's house. Her friend's parents stayed out of the way and let the girls have fun. Her friend suggested they chat with some boys online. Gianna's parents would not have approved. They had warned Gianna that chatting with strangers can lead to trouble. Gianna felt the Holy Spirit guiding her away from chatting, but she decided not to listen. She went along with her friend and talked with boys on social media. Afterward, Gianna felt guilty and even ashamed. She knew if she had obeyed the Holy Spirit, she wouldn't have those ugly feelings. The Holy Spirit allowed Gianna to feel them because she needed to remember how Jesus wanted her to behave. When you feel the Holy Spirit speaking to you, listen. Then do your best to obey.

Dear Jesus, it's hard sometimes to obey You when I want to follow my friends. Please give me courage to say no to whatever I know is wrong. Amen.

Gentleness

Let all people see how gentle you are.
The Lord is coming again soon.
PHILIPPIANS 4:5 NLV

What words can you think of to describe what it means to be gentle? Some dictionaries use words like *calm*, *kind*, *caring*, and *soft*. The Bible tells us Jesus is gentle. Jesus said, "Follow My teachings and learn from Me. I am gentle" (Matthew 11:29 NLV). Jesus cared deeply about people. He spoke softly and brought peace to those who were sick or hurting. He was helpful and kind. It feels good to be treated gently. When we treat others with gentleness, we use quiet, caring words. A soft touch or a warm hug can help someone's sadness go away. A simple act of kindness can bring someone a feeling of safety or peace. Gather up all your good feelings and use them to be gentle. It is one of the kindest things you can do to help others feel cared for and loved.

Lord, help me to grow in gentleness. Teach me to be gentle with actions and words and to bring caring and kindness wherever I go. Amen.

A Gentle Response

What do you want? Do you want me to come with a stick to whip you? Or do you want me to come with love and a gentle spirit?
1 CORINTHIANS 4:21 NLV

Gianna felt guilty for disobeying her parents and ashamed for disappointing God. She told God what she had done. She also confessed to her parents that she had done something they didn't approve of. Instead of using angry words and scolding Gianna, her dad calmly explained that the rules they set for her were there to protect her. He spoke gently, telling her that although he felt disappointed in her behavior, he was happy that she told them what she had done. Her dad responded in a gentle, loving way. Gianna learned from him that we can be both firm and gentle by choosing the words we say and how we say them. That's how Jesus reacted when He felt disappointed with someone—gently but firmly. Jesus used His words to teach and lead others to do what is right.

Jesus, when I need to deal with a difficult person or situation, guide me to respond with firm but gentle words. Amen.

Warm Fuzzies

Now you sincerely love each other.
But you must keep on loving with all your heart.
1 PETER 1:22 CEV

Have you ever given someone "warm fuzzies"? Don't worry, it's not a disease! And warm fuzzies can't be seen or touched like soft pj's or fluffy socks. We only feel them inside our hearts. They are the happy, contented feelings people get from being treated well. When we share with others our feelings of love, kindness, caring, understanding, and compassion, it's like giving them a gift. If they open their hearts to receive it, then their hearts fill up with good feelings too. They feel cared about and loved. What are some things you could do or say to give someone warm fuzzies? Saying "I love you," giving a compliment, encouraging someone, lending a helping hand, and surprising someone with a little gift are just a few ideas. Give it a try this week. Share your good feelings and make someone else feel good.

Dear God, You bless me every day with so many good feelings. I want to share them with others so they will feel good too. Amen.

The Best gift God gives us
is Jesus! No one can make
our hearts feel more loving
and joyful than He can.

More Warm Fuzzies

Thank God for His great Gift.
2 CORINTHIANS 9:15 NLV

What gives you the warm fuzzies? What makes you feel good or cared for and loved? God places things, animals, and people all around us to help us feel good. They are His gifts to us each day. Snuggling with our pets can give us a warm, fuzzy feeling. Enjoying our favorite foods can too. A beautiful scene can make us say, "Oh, wow!" and fill our hearts with awe. A good book, a cup of cocoa, joyful times spent with family and friends—they all bring us warm fuzzies. A hug, tender words, understanding, compassion, mercy, forgiveness—all these make us feel good inside. The best gift God gives us is Jesus! No one can make our hearts feel more loving and joyful than He can. The world is filled with God's warm, fuzzy gifts. We need to look for them using our senses and then open our hearts to receive them.

Thank You, God, for Your amazing and wonderful gifts. Open my eyes to see them. Open my ears to hear them. Open my heart to receive them. Amen.

Eyes That See

"Even then God did not leave you without something to see of Him. He did good."
ACTS 14:17 NLV

Talia saw some older boys being mean to the little boy who lived next door. They took his baseball cap and played catch with it. When the boy cried, they called him a baby. "Hey!" Talia shouted at them. "Leave him alone!" The boys ran away laughing. One of them threw the little boy's cap toward Talia. She picked it up and brought it to him. She put it on his head and said, "It's okay. You didn't deserve to be treated that way." What Talia saw had made her feel angry and even worried about the little boy. But comforting him and seeing him smile helped make Talia's ugly feelings go away. Sometimes what we see causes bad feelings, but God has a way of working things out so we see the good in Him. He had put Talia just where He needed her to comfort the little boy.

Heavenly Father, guide me to notice You at work in everything I see. Amen.

Ears That Hear

"You have ears, do you not hear? Do you not remember?"
MARK 8:18 NLV

What we hear connects with how we feel. Rose and her friends were listening to music. Some of the songs had swear words and other lyrics that weren't very nice. Rose felt uncomfortable listening. That uncomfortable feeling was the Holy Spirit reminding her that God didn't approve of that kind of language. Sometimes we have a choice about what we allow our ears to hear. We get to choose the music we listen to and the concerts we attend. When we have a choice, we should choose what brings honor to God. If, like Rose, you feel the Holy Spirit allowing you to feel uncomfortable with something you listen to, turn it off, choose something else, or simply walk away. Sometime when you and your family are relaxing together, talk about the music you listen to and enjoy. Decide if God approves.

Dear God, when I feel in my heart that the music I listen to doesn't bring You honor, please give me the courage to turn it off or walk away. Amen.

Taste. It's So Good!

O taste and see that the Lord is good.
How happy is the man who trusts in Him!
PSALM 34:8 NLV

A cold lemonade on a hot day helps us feel refreshed. Hot cider on a cold day helps us feel cozy. A favorite meal prepared in our honor helps us feel loved. Chicken soup feels comforting when we have a cold. If we try a food that we think we won't like, we feel brave. And if we do like it, we feel surprised. If we eat too much, then we feel sick! Taste connects with our feelings. God gives us all kinds of food to try—sweet, sour, bitter, salty, spicy. Be brave and taste some that are unfamiliar. See how they make you feel. Share food with others—a plate of homemade cookies for a neighbor, a bottle of cold water for the mail carrier, a sandwich for someone who is hungry. . . Sharing shows we care. It makes people feel appreciated and loved.

Father, You created our bodies perfectly, connecting our five senses to how we feel. Everything You do is amazing. Amen.

Thanks Be to God

He gives food to every creature. His love endures forever.
Psalm 136:25 NIV

The Bible tells of God's people, the Israelites, walking through the desert after escaping from slavery in Egypt. God had provided them with a daring rescue, and He promised them a new homeland. But on the way, in the desert, the people felt hungry, so hungry they were starving. There was nothing to eat. God rained down from heaven bread for them. It tasted like wafers made with honey. He provided quails as meat for them to eat. They took just enough for each day, and the food kept them fed for forty years until they reached the Promised Land. God's kindness had relieved their feelings of hunger and kept them from starving to death. Today God still provides food for the hungry. It doesn't rain down from heaven, but it comes from kind people who feel caring and compassionate and share what they have. God provides all the food we eat. Do you remember to thank Him? Get in the habit of praying before each meal.

Lord God, thank You for the food I eat and for all Your blessings. Amen.

What's That Smell?

Oil and perfume make the heart glad.
PROVERBS 27:9 NLV

The Bible says the wise men brought to baby Jesus gifts of comforting, sweet-smelling frankincense and myrrh. The sense of smell is another of God's amazing gifts. The scent of roses in springtime, the way the earth smells after a summer rain, turkey roasting at Thanksgiving, pine trees at Christmastime—good smells give us warm, welcome feelings. Some scents we will remember for the rest of our lives because they connect with memories of loved ones and happy times spent together. Other scents are like alarm bells that warn us of danger: Don't let the dog out; there's a skunk nearby. Something is burning on the stove! Did you take out the trash? Good smells make us feel cozy, joyful, refreshed, and relaxed and remind us of good things. Bad smells connect with feelings of awareness and fear and can even make us sick. What are some of your favorite smells? How do they make you feel?

Lord, speak to my heart through my senses. Make me even more aware of how they connect with my feelings. Amen.

A Soft, Caring Touch

She said to herself, "If I only touch the bottom of His coat, I will be healed."
MATTHEW 9:21 NLV

God blesses each of us with the ability to touch and feel. When wrapped in a soft, fluffy blanket, we feel cozy and warm. On a hot day, running through a sprinkler's ice-cold water feels a little shocking, but it quickly cools us down. A gentle hand on a feverish forehead makes us feel cared for. A hug makes us feel loved. Even our pets enjoy a soft, caring touch. Cats react with a purr when petted, and dogs shove our hands with their wet noses, wanting to be petted some more. When Jesus lived on earth, people wanted to touch Him. His touch was so powerful it could heal the sick. Today Jesus' comforting presence is all around us like a big, gentle hug. We can feel Him in every soft, caring touch.

Lord Jesus, help me to feel nearer to You through my sense of touch. Open my heart to feel Your presence in the sunshine's warmth, a cool breeze, or a gentle hug. Amen.

I Feel Brokenhearted

The Lord is near to those who have a broken heart. And He saves those who are broken in spirit.
PSALM 34:18 NLV

The one word that best described how Avery felt when her beloved dog, Toby, passed away, is *brokenhearted*. An empty and sad feeling now occupied the space Toby had filled with love and joy. Avery didn't think she would ever heal. Her heart felt too broken. Losing a person or a pet we love can break our heart. So can disappointment or being picked on or rejected. The first broken heart is part of growing up. Everyone will feel heartache. When it happens, God is nearby, wanting to help. If you ask Him to come into your broken heart, He will fill it with His love and heal it. It is one of those things that takes time, though. Just as our bodies take time to heal when they hurt, healing a heartache takes time too.

Dear heavenly Father, I feel so very sad. Please come into my broken heart and heal it. Amen.

PSALM 34:18

The Lord is near to those who have a broken heart. And He saves those who are broken in spirit.

Oh-So-Big

Hurry to help me, O Lord, Who saves me!
PSALM 38:22 NLV

When big things happen, it's normal to have big feelings. It's normal to feel brokenhearted when you lose a loved one. If someone tries to hurt you or something big happens that you don't deserve, it's normal to feel outraged. If you suddenly find yourself in a dangerous situation, it's normal to feel terrified. When ugly, oh-so-big feelings happen suddenly, the first thing to do is call on God. That's what King David did in Psalm 38:22. He said, "Hurry to help me, O Lord, Who saves me!" Pray and ask God to save you. Ask Him to bring people near you to help. Then trust God to help and do your best to be brave. After David prayed, he said, "My soul. . .waits for God alone. . . . He is my strong place. I will not be shaken" (Psalm 62:5–6 NLV). When big things happen, God is with you wherever you go. He will never leave you alone.

Lord, save me! Help me to be brave until these oh-so-big feelings go away. Amen.

Waaaaay Too Big!

O Lord, save me from lying lips and a false tongue.
PSALM 120:2 NLV

When Petra felt even a tiny bit angry, sad, disappointed, or sick, her reaction was way too big. When angry, she stamped her foot and shouted, "I hate this!" If something disappointed Petra, she pouted and said, "I didn't deserve this." When sad, she cried and wailed at the top of her lungs. And when she felt just a little sick, Petra said, "I'm dying!" Petra lied about her feelings. She liked the attention she got by pretending they were big. Still, when people realized Petra was overreacting, they found her behavior, well, *annoying*! The Bible says a lot about lying. God hates lies. He wants us to be truthful about everything including our feelings. When something causes us to feel sad, angry, sick, or disappointed, we should ask ourselves, "How bad is this really?" and then shift our attention to turning those bad feelings around.

Lord, whether it's about my feelings or anything else, if I feel like exaggerating or lying, please speak to my heart and remind me to tell the truth. Amen.

Whatever I Want!

Some of you say, "We can do anything we want to." But I tell you not everything is good for us. So I refuse to let anything have power over me.
1 CORINTHIANS 6:12 CEV

Gabby disliked her parents' rules. She thought they were silly. The resentment she felt spilled out in disrespect when she told her mother, "I'm old enough to do whatever I want!" She pretended not to care when her mom punished her for talking back. *Arrogant* describes Gabby's behavior. She felt she knew better than her mother, and that led to disrespect. Had Gabby thought about it, she would have known that arrogant behavior is not pleasing to God. First Corinthians 6:12 is a reminder that not everything is good for us. Rules are set to help us. When feelings of arrogance and disrespect try to enter our hearts, we have the power to say no and get rid of those feelings right away.

Dear God, I know my parents make rules to keep me safe and teach me how to behave. Please help me let go of any arrogant feelings and to be respectful. Amen.

Stuck-up

Nothing should be done because of pride or thinking about yourself. Think of other people as more important than yourself.
PHILIPPIANS 2:3 NLV

There are words for people who believe they are better than others: *conceited*, *snobbish*, *selfish*, *arrogant*, *stuck-up*, and *prideful*. When people think they are all that, it would be wise for them to obey what Philippians 2:3 says. Jesus' follower Paul wrote that verse, and he was echoing something Jesus said in Luke 14:11 (NLV): "Whoever makes himself look more important than he is will find out how little he is worth. Whoever does not try to honor himself will be made important." Self-importance is an ugly feeling and one to get rid of. When we learn to think of others as being more important than ourselves, we become more giving, compassionate, and caring. How do you feel around someone who is stuck-up? Do you think that person builds you up or cuts you down?

Dear Jesus, thank You for teaching me to get rid of my ugly, prideful feelings and instead to care about others and put their needs first. Amen.

Prideful or Proud?

Whatever work you do, do it with all your heart. Do it for the Lord and not for men.
COLOSSIANS 3:23 NLV

Pride is a tricky feeling. It can be ugly or good. Being prideful is the selfish feeling that we are more important than others. But pride can be a good thing when it means we are pleased with the result of our work. The Bible says whatever we do, we should do it as if we are serving God. When we do our very best, it makes God proud, and that should make us feel proud too. It is important to give God the credit for our good work because He gives us the skill and talent to get the job done. We feel proud to serve God and know that He trusts us to do His work here on earth. It is okay to feel proud, but not prideful, of the good work you do.

Dear Lord, I want to do my best work because I know it makes You proud of me. I'm proud to serve You in all that I do. Amen.

Self-Control

Losing self-control leaves you as helpless as a city without a wall.
PROVERBS 25:28 CEV

Self-control means not allowing your feelings to explode. If someone said something mean to you in the lunchroom, would you stand up in front of everyone and shout, cry, or, worse, hit the person who insulted you? That would be allowing your feelings to get way out of control. If you were at a party and someone offered you a food you didn't like, would you shove it away and yell, "No! No! No!"? Losing control of yourself can make you feel embarrassed. It's like a big spotlight shines on you and everyone looks and wonders *What's up with that girl?* You have self-control when you take charge of your thoughts, words, and actions. The Holy Spirit helps with that. When you hear Him saying inside your heart, "Calm down," then it's wise to stop, say a silent prayer, and think before you say or do something you might regret.

Father in heaven, I want to keep my emotions under control. When it feels like they might explode, please remind me to stop, pray, and calm down. Amen.

Spilled Feelings

Do not act like the sinful people of the world. Let God change your life. First of all, let Him give you a new mind. Then you will know what God wants you to do. And the things you do will be good and pleasing and perfect.

ROMANS 12:2 NLV

Ivy had a bad day at school. She held her feelings in until she got home. Then she lost control. Her ugly feelings spilled all over the place. "Don't talk to me!" she snapped at her brother. When her mom asked what was wrong, Ivy said, "I don't want to talk about it." She went to her room, closed the door, lay on her bed, and cried. Meltdowns don't need to happen if our goal is to please God. Ivy could have chased away those ugly feelings by asking God to give her a new mind. She could have slowly let out those feelings instead of allowing them to build. When everything goes wrong, think about God. Ask yourself, "What can I do to please God?"

Lord, help me to keep my ugly feelings from spilling out. I want to please You with my actions and thoughts. Amen.

Spoiled Feelings

Put out of your life all these things:
bad feelings about other people, anger, temper,
loud talk, bad talk which hurts other people,
and bad feelings which hurt other people.
EPHESIANS 4:31 NLV

Have you ever smelled spoiled milk? One whiff and, "Eww! It stinks." Milk that has been hanging around too long smells. It's something you want to get rid of. If you drank it, yuck! Feelings that hang around too long can get spoiled too. They can make our attitude stink. If anger, disappointment, and hurt last a long time and if they fill you all the time with stinky feelings, then it's time to ask for help. Ask God to help you get rid of those feelings and also ask your parents, pastor, teacher, or another trusted adult. We all need help sometimes to know where our smelly feelings are coming from so we can throw them out. Ask for help when you need it.

Dear God, these ugly feelings have been with me way too long. I want to get rid of them. Please lead me to whatever kind of help I need. Amen.

I Feel Guilty

Jesus said, "If you were blind, you would not be guilty of sin; but now that you claim you can see, your guilt remains."
JOHN 9:41 NIV

Brittany knew it was wrong to turn in her brother's essay as her own. Afterward, she had all sorts of weird feelings—anxiety, fear, regret, worry, shame, sadness. If Brittany had to condense all those feelings into one word, it would be *guilt*. What she did made her feel guilty. It wasn't right to pretend that she had written that essay. Brittany knew it hadn't pleased God. The only way to make her guilt go away was to tell her teacher the truth and apologize. It wasn't easy, but she did it. Brittany wrote her own essay. She took it to her teacher and confessed what she had done. Brittany asked her teacher to forgive her. She asked God to forgive her too. She knew God would forgive her, and she hoped her teacher would too. She promised them both that she would never do it again.

Lord, I feel guilty. What I did was wrong. Please forgive me and help me to make things right. Amen.

My Conscience

Dear friends, if our heart does not say that we are wrong, we will have no fear as we stand before [God].
1 JOHN 3:21 NLV

What if you aren't sure if something is right or wrong? Your conscience will let you know. It is that inner feeling that guides you. Your conscience is actually the Holy Spirit. It is God's voice inside your heart warning you to be careful, to wait, or to change direction. God knows what you are thinking. If you are heading in the wrong direction, He will say so in your heart, and He might allow you to feel a little afraid or worried about what you plan to do. If God doesn't tell you that it's wrong, then you shouldn't feel worried or afraid. Learn to listen to your heart, and if you still aren't sure, give it more thought. Read your Bible and ask God to guide you. He will never send you in the wrong direction.

Dear God, sometimes I'm not sure if something is right or wrong. Teach me to listen to my heart and to hear Your voice. Guide me in the way I should go. Amen.

1 JOHN 3:20

Our heart may say that we have done wrong. But remember, God is greater than our heart. He knows everything.

Another voice

Our heart may say that we have done wrong. But remember, God is greater than our heart. He knows everything.
1 JOHN 3:20 NLV

God isn't the only one who speaks to our hearts. Satan does too. In this book, you have read about girls who felt worried, guilty, embarrassed, or ashamed when they hadn't done anything wrong. Satan likes to tell us that things are our fault when they're not. For example, he is the one who makes us feel embarrassed if, like Mindy, we forget our lines in a play. He says it's our fault if our parents don't get along or if we can't solve the problems in our family. God knows when Satan speaks to our hearts, and His voice is way more powerful than Satan's. God will tell you when you've done nothing wrong. He will lead you away from false guilt, embarrassment, and shame. Think about it. Do you recognize Satan's voice in your heart? How is it different from God's?

God, teach me to recognize Satan's voice, and lead me away from false feelings of shame, embarrassment, and guilt. Amen.

I Feel Aware

I have placed the Lord always in front of me.
Because He is at my right hand, I will not be moved.
PSALM 16:8 NLV

Whitney enjoyed camping with her dad and her older brother, Jake. Her dad knew a lot about surviving in the wild, and he taught Whitney and Jake to be aware of their surroundings. When they camped in the woods, Whitney learned to be still and listen for sounds. She learned to be aware of food, like berries, that were safe to eat. Her dad taught them to be aware of where they had come from, where they were, and where they were going. Most important, he taught Whitney and Jake to always be aware that God was with them. Awareness is a feeling we want to grow. It helps keep us out of trouble and safe wherever we go. How aware are you of what's happening around you? Practice using your senses to become more aware.

Lord, often I'm too busy with other things to think about what's going on around me. Help me to become more aware, especially if trouble is heading my way. Amen.

Look Around

Take notice, you senseless ones among the people; you fools, when will you become wise?
PSALM 94:8 NIV

How aware are you of what's going on with your family members and friends? It is important to look around and notice how others are feeling. The Bible says it is wise to "take notice." If you grow the feeling of awareness, then the feeling of compassion—concern for the troubles of others—will grow along with it. If you are aware when something is troubling others, then you can help by being compassionate and caring. Awareness is a way we show love toward others. As you look around and notice what others are doing, the Holy Spirit might say inside your heart, "That person needs some attention; help her," or "Your baby sister is about to run across the street; take her hand." It is wise to grow awareness because it often results in something good. Can you think of a time when being aware led you to help someone?

Heavenly Father, guide me to notice the people around me and to be aware of their feelings. Then lead me to help whenever I can. Amen.

Things I Really, Really Love

Never give up. Eagerly follow the Holy Spirit and serve the Lord.
ROMANS 12:11 CEV

Passion is a word that describes a super strong feeling about something. Passion can't stand alone. It always connects with another feeling, usually love. For example, if you really, *really* love skating, then you are passionate about it. You can feel passion for just about anything—a kind of food, a hobby, an idea, fitness, reading, learning a new skill, even people! If you have really strong feelings about something, those feelings will lead you to hang on to what you love and not give up. The best thing to feel passionate about is loving and serving God. Often, He will take a person's passion for something and make it grow. Think about all the great inventions in the world. Each began with someone's passion to create, and that led to something good. What are you passionate about? What do you really, *really* love?

Dear God, when I think about it, I realize there are many things that I really, really love. Please take my passion for the best of them and help me to create something good. Amen.

Share Your Passion

Let us help each other to love others and to do good.
HEBREWS 10:24 NLV

Passion is a feeling that connects us with friends. If we feel passionate about an idea or a cause, we can get involved with others in our churches, schools, and communities to do something good. Aurora felt passionate about helping the homeless shelters in her community. She and her youth group at church raised funds to buy supplies for care boxes. Together they packed boxes with things people staying in a shelter might need. They also asked their church members to contribute warm, gently used coats, new socks, gloves, hats, and scarves. Aurora's passion for the homeless went a long way to help those in her community. Are you involved in sharing your passion with others? Join a group or form one yourself. Have fun and use your passion to bring goodness to the world.

Lord, You know the things I feel passionate about. I don't want to keep my passion all to myself. Please guide me to others who share my feelings. Then help us to bring some goodness to the world. Amen.

When Passion Turns Ugly

Do not have anything to do with a man given to anger, or go with a man who has a bad temper.
PROVERBS 22:24 NLV

Passion is a feeling that can get out of control in a bad way. If we aren't careful, it can lead to anger. People can become so passionate about what they believe in that they feel rage—out of control anger—when things don't go their way. When joining with others who share your passionate feelings, be careful that your passion doesn't turn ugly. There are those who vent their anger by making fun of others and wanting to hurt them. Some try to get rid of their anger by damaging or destroying property. The Bible warns us in Proverbs 22:24 not to have anything to do with those people. When God gives us passion to change something or help someone, He wants us to use our passionate feelings in a good way.

Father, if ever I notice my feelings of passion turning to anger, I will know it is a warning from You to stop and use my passion to help people and do something good. Amen.

I Feel Adventurous

You will show me the way of life. Being with You is to be full of joy. In Your right hand there is happiness forever.
PSALM 16:11 NLV

Danica was passionate about adventure. She loved new and exciting experiences. She loved trying challenging sports like obstacle courses and rock-climbing walls. She was never afraid to sample foods from different countries and cultures. And when her family went on vacation, Danica was the first one to suggest an adventure to an out-of-the-way place they could explore together. Danica's adventurous feelings led her to dream of her future—places she wanted to go, things she wanted to do, and the people she might meet along the way who shared her passion. Danica didn't know it yet, but God had all kinds of adventures planned for her future, adventures that would bring her joy and happiness forever. How adventurous do you feel? Make a list of some places you want to go and things you want to do.

Dear God, please grow my adventurous feelings. Lead me to new experiences that will fill my life with happiness and joy. Amen.

I Feel Daring

[Christ's] power at work in us can do far more than we dare ask or imagine.

EPHESIANS 3:21 CEV

Fiona played a game of *I Dare You*. She dared herself to reach goals that were hard to imagine. Fiona said to herself, "I dare you to bring your math grade from a C to an A," and she did it. She dared herself to overcome her fear of heights. With a little help from her dad, she did that too. Playing the *I Dare You* game gave Fiona courage to try new things. Always, before she dared herself to reach for a goal, Fiona talked with Jesus about it. She knew that His power working in her would guide her to do way more than she imagined. And if the goal Fiona planned wasn't right for her, she trusted the Holy Spirit to tell her and lead her in a different direction. Do you feel daring? Pray about the goals you would like to reach. If you feel Jesus saying yes, then dare yourself to try.

Dear Jesus, please let Your power work within me to help me reach my goals. Amen.

"Don't You Dare!"

The wise see danger ahead and avoid it,
but fools keep going and get into trouble.
PROVERBS 27:12 NCV

Daring is best friends with another feeling—Wisdom. Daring and Wisdom work together to help us make good choices. Some dares are okay, like when Fiona dared herself to bring up her math grade and to overcome her fear of heights. But other dares can lead to danger. If a kid at your school dared you to smoke or take drugs, Wisdom would shout, "Don't you dare!" You know to listen to your heart, be wise, notice danger, and avoid it. If you dared to swim alone, especially where there were no lifeguards, that would be foolish. If you dared to take a ride from a stranger, that would be foolish too. Each time you use your feelings to act with wisdom, God is pleased. What are some other situations you can think of when Wisdom would say, "Don't you dare"?

Heavenly Father, if I feel even a tiny bit like doing something daring that I know is dangerous, remind me to be wise and just say no. Amen.

I Feel Free

The heart is free where the Spirit of the Lord is. The Lord is the Spirit.
2 CORINTHIANS 3:17 NLV

One of God's greatest gifts is freedom. Beginning with Adam and Eve, the first humans on earth, God gave people freedom to make their own choices. He gave Adam and Eve a perfect world to live in with just one rule: "You are free to eat from any tree of the garden. But do not eat from the tree of learning of good and bad" (Genesis 2:16–17 NLV). It didn't take long before Adam and Eve chose to disobey. They ate the fruit. When they made that choice, it unleashed sin into the world forever. Still, God continued allowing people freedom to choose. If we don't use our freedom wisely and we choose sin, we are inviting Satan to come into our lives and mess things up. But when we combine our freedom with wise choices, we please God and He opens our hearts to good feelings, like happiness and peace.

Lord, thank You for allowing me the freedom to choose. Please guide me to make wise choices that will please You. Amen.

When we combine our
freedom with wise choices,
we please God and He opens
our hearts to good feelings,
like happiness and peace.

I Feel Safe

Yes, God kept us from what looked like sure death and He is keeping us. As we trust Him, He will keep us in the future.
2 CORINTHIANS 1:10 NLV

In the Bible, you will find stories about men who faced danger yet felt safe knowing God was with them. When a king's edict forbade Daniel to pray to God, Daniel chose not to obey because he knew it was right to pray to God. Daniel was punished by being put into a den with hungry lions. God went with him, and Daniel survived without a scratch (Daniel, chapter 6). Shadrach, Meshach, and Abednego refused to bow to a false god, so the king threw them into a fiery furnace. God went with them too, and the men survived without a burn (Daniel 3:8–25). There are many great stories of people who felt safe with God. If ever you face danger, you can feel safe knowing God is with you. He is taking care of you right now, and He will be with you and care for you forever.

Father God, I trust You to take care of me, and I feel safe knowing You are with me. Amen.

Have Faith

[Jesus] said to them, "Why are you afraid? You have so little faith!"
MATTHEW 8:26 NLV

Faith is when we have complete trust in Jesus. When we have faith, we feel safe and strong knowing Jesus is with us. Kaylee was at sleepover camp. Late one night, when most girls in her dorm were asleep, Kaylee heard thunder rumbling in the distance. She didn't want anyone to know that storms terrified her, and she felt even more afraid if they happened in the dark. She could feel her heart pounding and she felt like sobbing. But then Kaylee remembered what Jesus said to His disciples when they felt afraid of a storm: "Why are you afraid? You have so little faith!" Then Jesus calmed the storm. Kaylee said a silent prayer, and she did her best to have faith that Jesus would protect her from the storm. Jesus wants us to build our feelings of faith. Strong faith in Him keeps us from feeling afraid.

Dear Jesus, please help me build up my feelings of faith. I trust You, but I want to trust You even more. Amen.

God Is Faithful

Your love, LORD, reaches to the heavens,
your faithfulness to the skies.
PSALM 36:5 NIV

God's faithfulness to us isn't just big—it's huge! His faithfulness reaches the sky and beyond what we can see or imagine. The Bible says we can trust in God's faithfulness. That means we can always depend on Him. God is faithful in keeping all His promises. His feelings of love, grace, and mercy for us will never end. All His goodness and the wonderful ways He cares for us will never change. We can trust God all the time. God's faithfulness helps build our faith in Him. When we think about His great power and His love for us, our feelings of faith increase. As our faith increases, so do our feelings of peace, trust, and strength. Faith in God leads us to feel courageous and brave, especially in trouble, because we know God will protect us. What are some ways God has been faithful to you?

Your never-ending and unchanging faithfulness and love for me make me feel protected and safe. Thank You, God! Amen.

Big, Bigger, Biggest

Through God we will do valiantly, for it is He who shall tread down our enemies.
PSALM 60:12 NKJV

Feelings come in different sizes. The words we choose to describe them can show how big they are. For example, we feel *brave*. We can describe a bigger feeling of brave as *courageous*. A word for a really big, brave feeling is *valiant*. A valiant feeling means we are ready to face trouble by setting aside our feelings of fear. We are like soldiers marching into battle. In the Bible, God's soldiers had so much faith in Him that they went into war feeling valiant. They felt really brave knowing that God was with them. His soldiers were sure God would help them win the battle. Faith in God grows feelings of bravery while it shrinks feelings of fear. If you can build a small brave feeling into a valiant feeling, then you can fight any kind of trouble because you know God will lead you.

Dear God, teach me to face trouble valiantly by putting all my trust in Your faithfulness, power, and love. Amen.

I Feel Ecstatic!

Show your happiness, all peoples!
Call out to God with the voice of joy! . . .
He is a great King over all the earth.
PSALM 47:1–2 NLV

Happiness is another feeling we can describe as big, bigger, and biggest. A little happiness makes us feel pleased. When happiness grows, it becomes a joyous feeling. When a joyous feeling grows, it can overflow into joyfulness that gushes out all over the place, making us feel ecstatic—a sudden, very powerful feeling of joy. Rachael felt pleased knowing her cousin might come to stay for the summer. She felt joyous when her cousin said she could come. And when Rachael saw her cousin arrive at the airport, she felt ecstatic. God loves watching our happiness grow. His wonderful blessings make us feel ecstatic. When God blesses you with something good, tell people. Let them see your happiness. Let it shine like a bright light that leads others to Him.

Lord, Your blessings make me happy. Your never-ending goodness makes me feel ecstatic. I will tell others how happy You make me, and I pray my words will lead them nearer to You. Amen.

Think About It

Let the wise man think about these things. And may he think about the loving-kindness of the Lord.
PSALM 107:43 NLV

Thinking about your feelings helps get rid of those that are ugly and build those that are good. There are so many feelings, and they come in different sizes. When you feel a feeling, give it a name. Then decide how big it is. Is it just a little feeling—tiny, microscopic? Is it really big—gigantic, huge, humongous? Or maybe it's somewhere in between? Go to your quiet place and think about the feelings listed on this page. Think about a time you felt each one. Then describe how it felt and how big the feeling was.

Anger	Fear
Sadness	Hurt
Happiness	Embarrassment

Did you find any really big feelings? Did you discover you can have more than one feeling at a time?

Lord, when I think about my emotions, I think about You. You care about how I feel. I know You will help me with any feelings that aren't good. Amen.

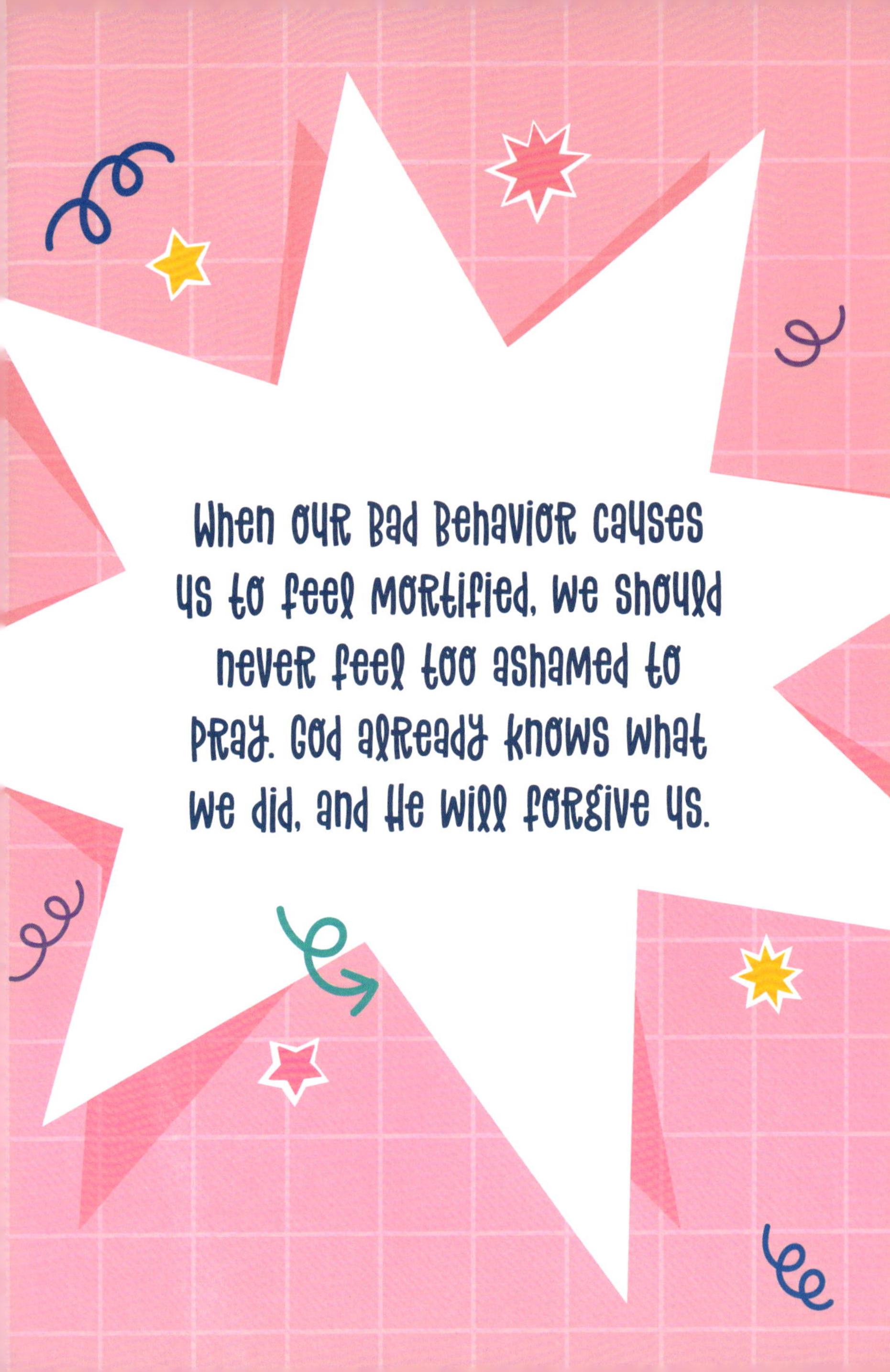
When our bad behavior causes us to feel mortified, we should never feel too ashamed to pray. God already knows what we did, and He will forgive us.

I Feel Mortified!

I prayed, "My God, I am too ashamed and embarrassed to lift up my face to you."
EZRA 9:6 NCV

There are so many feelings and even more words to describe them. Maybe you have discovered some new words to express exactly how you feel. *Mortified* is a word that means "extremely embarrassed." If a kid's pants fell down in class, he would feel mortified! If you were in your sister's wedding and stumbled and fell while walking down the aisle, you would feel mortified. Some things that cause us to feel mortified are out of our control. Others are not. In the Bible, Ezra prayed on behalf of the Israelites who had been behaving badly. Ezra told God he felt almost too ashamed and embarrassed to pray, but still Ezra prayed, asking God for forgiveness. When our bad behavior causes us to feel mortified, we should never feel too ashamed to pray. God already knows what we did, and He will forgive us.

Dear God, I feel so ashamed—mortified—
for the way I behaved, and I'm sorry.
Please forgive me. Amen.

Do Tell?

O Lord, put a watch over my mouth.
Keep watch over the door of my lips.
PSALM 141:3 NLV

It is right to be honest about your feelings, but that doesn't mean you have to tell everyone exactly why you feel as you do. Sometimes it's best not to tell. If the reason you feel a certain way is something you want to keep private, then keep it to yourself. If you don't want to tell because you might hurt someone's feelings, you can keep that to yourself too. It's okay to say something like "I feel angry, but I don't want to talk about it right now." There are some things you might only want to tell God. But—this is important—if someone hurts you or if you feel in any kind of danger, you must tell a grown-up why you feel as you do. And talk to your parents or a safe adult if you feel very sad and the sadness won't go away. Telling a safe adult like a teacher, a counselor, or your parents will help to keep you safe.

Lord, guide me to know what to reveal about my feelings. Give me courage to tell my parents about any big feelings that are scary or sad. Amen.

Enchanted, My Dear

"Have no gods other than Me."
EXODUS 20:3 NLV

In fairy tales, a spell is sometimes put on a princess to enchant her—to shift all her attention to someone or something. It might be a problem the princess has to overcome, or maybe it's something good, like finding her Prince Charming. Stories entertain us, but we need to be careful about any real feelings of enchantment. Satan tries to pull us away from God by getting us to focus on our troubles or to love something or someone more than we love God. Anything at all that shifts all our attention away from God enchants us and becomes an "idol." An idol is like a little god that we greatly admire and worship by giving it all our attention. God says, "Have no gods other than Me." God wants all our attention, time, and love. If you notice anything beginning to pull your feelings away from Him, break that spell. Put God first in everything you think, say, and do.

Heavenly Father, please protect me from anything that shifts my feelings away from You. I want You to be my everything. Amen.

Talk About It

Pour out your feelings to the Lord,
as you would pour water out of a jug.
LAMENTATIONS 2:19 CEV

Talk with God about your feelings. Tell Him how big your feelings are and what they feel like. God already knows your feelings, but He also knows that talking about them helps. Talking gets your feelings out so they won't stay all bottled up inside you. You don't want ugly feelings getting all stale in there and growing! It's important to talk about your feelings with your parents and others you trust. When you talk with family members and friends about big feelings, you will discover you aren't alone. Everyone has feelings, and most people have experienced big, unpleasant feelings. What was your biggest feeling today? Whether it was a good feeling or an ugly feeling, tell God about it. Name that feeling and tell God how it felt.

Dear God, sometimes I don't talk about my feelings because I don't have the right words to describe them. Still, I know that however I describe my feelings to You, You will understand. Amen.

Be Honest

"He that is not honest with little things is not honest with big things."
LUKE 16:10 NLV

Ashley kept her feelings to herself. She didn't want others to know when big, ugly feelings were lurking inside her. If someone asked, "How are you doing?" Ashley would answer, "Fine." But she wasn't fine. Keeping her big feelings inside was like carrying an elephant on her back! It zapped Ashley's energy and stole her happiness. If she had been honest about her ugly feelings, Ashley might have found some understanding, compassion, and help getting rid of them. Whether an ugly feeling is small and you think it's not worth discussing, or big and embarrassing and you're ashamed of it, be honest. Tell God how you really feel. He already knows, and He will forgive anything you have done wrong. Be honest with your parents too. They love you and will help you.

Dear God, although You want me to be honest about everything, I don't have to tell everyone every detail about why I feel a certain way, but I will always be truthful about how I feel. Amen.

On Cloud Nine

If you are cheerful, you feel good.
PROVERBS 17:22 CEV

We often use informal words and phrases to describe our feelings. For example, Marissa was on "cloud nine" when she received an invitation to the dance. Can you guess what "cloud nine" means? If you guessed extremely happy, you are right. Marissa was extremely happy when she received an invitation to the dance. In the early twentieth century, clouds were assigned numbers based on their heights. The highest clouds were cloud nine. Since then, people have expressed happiness by using phrases like "I was on cloud nine!" It's a good feeling that comes as a result of a blessing. God is the one who blesses us with good things that make us feel extremely happy—reaching a goal, hearing good news, receiving an unexpected surprise or a special gift. These are several ways God blesses us with happy feelings. Can you think of others? Remember to give thanks to God for your blessings.

Father God, You are so good to me. The special ways You bless me make me feel like I'm on cloud nine. Thank You! Amen.

I Feel Blessed

Praise the God and Father of our Lord Jesus Christ for the spiritual blessings that Christ has brought us from heaven!
EPHESIANS 1:3 CEV

When Terry opened the front door, her dog, Muffin, squeezed past her and raced toward the street. A man walking by scooped up Muffin before she reached the curb and ran into traffic. When he returned Muffin to Terry, she said, "I feel so lucky you were there. Thank you!" We often use the word *lucky* when we receive something good, but luck has nothing to do with it. Every good thing is a blessing that comes from God. He is the one who sees everything, watches over us, and blesses us with His goodness. So, instead of saying, "I feel lucky," get in the habit of saying, "I feel blessed." Those words bring honor to God and give Him credit for everything good you receive.

Lord God, I will remember that good things don't come to me because I am lucky. Every good thing is a blessing that comes from You. Today and every day I feel blessed by Your goodness. Amen.

Frazzled

When my worry is great within me,
Your comfort brings joy to my soul.
PSALM 94:19 NLV

Brianna worried about everything—her grades, her appearance, whether people liked her, social situations—if there was anything that could be worried about, Brianna found a way to worry. She was worried about so many things that she felt frazzled. *Frazzled* is a word that describes how we feel when our worries make us tired. Brianna felt worn out from worrying and from losing sleep over her concerns. Maybe, like Brianna, you are a frazzled worrier. To get rid of that ugly feeling, try giving all your worries to Jesus. He will take them and comfort you so you can rest. Jesus has already worked out everything you are worrying about. Jesus is all-powerful, and He can handle everyone's worries without feeling frazzled. What worries can you give to Him today?

Dear Jesus, sometimes I get so frazzled over my worries that I forget You already have them under control. Today I feel worried about [fill in the blank]. Please take my worries and comfort me. Amen.

Bedazzled

Do not let anyone fool you. Bad people can make those who want to live good become bad.
1 CORINTHIANS 15:33 NLV

Ashley thought her parents were too strict. She imagined breaking their rules and doing whatever she wanted. Ashley admired an older girl in her school who broke rules all the time and got away with it. Her admiration for the girl grew bigger and bigger, and as it did Ashley felt even more willing to break her parents' rules. She felt bedazzled by the girl who behaved badly. *Bedazzled* is another word to describe a feeling of fascination. It is a big feeling that can separate us from God. The Bible says to be careful of the people we admire, the company we keep, and not be fooled by a person's behavior. If you feel totally in awe of—bedazzled by—someone, don't let that feeling pull you away from God and doing what's right.

Dear God, I want my feelings to lead me nearer to You. Help me not to become bedazzled by people I admire, especially those who behave badly. Amen.

Heavyhearted

God gives comfort to those whose hearts are heavy.
2 CORINTHIANS 7:6 NLV

Samantha's family was going through hard times. A family member was sick in the hospital, Samantha's dad had just lost his job, and her family was about to welcome a new baby, the sixth of Samantha's siblings. Samantha was the oldest. She wished she could fix all her family's troubles, but she couldn't, and that made Samantha heavyhearted—very sad and depressed. A heavyhearted feeling is one that likes to settle into our hearts and lie there for a while. Jesus knows what a heavy heart feels like, and He wants to comfort those who have heavy hearts. Maybe you have a friend whose family is going through a hard time. You can help ease her heavy heart by asking Jesus to comfort her. Along with that, you can be there for your friend to listen, help if you can, and let her know that Jesus loves her and you do too.

Dear Lord Jesus, please comfort my friend, and heal her heavy heart. Guide me to help her however I can. Amen.

2 CORINTHIANS 7:6

God gives comfort to those whose hearts are heavy.

Good Vibes

I said to the Lord, "You are my Lord.
All the good things I have come from You."
PSALM 16:2 NLV

Belle's dad was injured in an accident at work, and he was recovering in the hospital. A friend texted Belle, "I'm sending you good vibes." *Good vibes* is another way of saying "good feelings." Have you ever tried sending someone a feeling? You can't! Only God can do that. King David, who wrote Psalm 16, understood that everything good, including his feelings, came from God. If you know someone who is going through a difficult time, instead of saying, "I'm sending you good vibes" or "I'm wishing you the best," say something like "I promise to pray for you." Don't be shy about letting others know they can trust God to help and comfort them. Praying for people connects them directly with God, and that's something good vibes and wishes can't do.

Dear God, thank You for helping me find the right words to say when someone is going through trouble. I can't send them vibes, but I can send You a prayer. Amen.

I Feel All-Overish

God is not a God of confusion but a God of peace.
1 CORINTHIANS 14:33 NCV

How would you imagine someone feels if they told you, "I feel all-overish"? *All-overish* is an unusual word that means feeling a bit uneasy about what might happen in the future. It is one of those feelings that isn't easy to describe. One way to describe an all-overish feeling is that you feel restless. In the Bible, a young woman named Ruth was feeling uneasy and restless, wondering whether the handsome Boaz would decide to marry her. When Naomi noticed Ruth's all-overish feeling, she said, "Wait, my daughter, until you find out what happens" (Ruth 3:18 NIV). When we feel uneasy about what might happen, all we can do is wait patiently and have faith in God. He already knows what will happen. God wants to take a confused all-overish feeling and change it to a feeling of peace.

Father God, I'm feeling a little all-overish today, and I don't know why. Please take this restless, uneasy feeling and help me to find some peace. Amen.

Burned-Out

The Lord said, "I Myself will go with you. I will give you rest."
EXODUS 33:14 NLV

Paige put a load of clothes in the dryer and sat on the floor, looking through the glass window as they tumbled round and round. *That's sort of how I feel,* Paige thought. Whenever her mom worked a double shift, Paige helped with more of the chores at home. Some big feelings had been tumbling around inside her for so long that Paige felt *burned-out*. That's a word that describes the tiredness we experience when our feelings get too big. Round and round our feelings go until we're ready to collapse on our beds and say, "Enough already!" That's how Paige felt. As she sat there, Paige had a long talk with God. She felt more relaxed as she remembered His words in Exodus 33:14: "I will give you rest." God always keeps His promises. If your feelings are big and you feel burned-out, go to Him. Ask Him to help you relax.

Dear God, I feel burned-out. Too much is going on, and I just want it all to go away. Please comfort me and give me rest. Amen.

Refreshed, Rejuvenated, Renewed

"I will refresh the weary and satisfy the faint."
JEREMIAH 31:25 NIV

A cool hand on a feverish forehead, a fresh breeze, a swim in the pool on a hot day, spending time in nature, reading a good book, relaxing while you listen to music—all of these can help to refresh you when you feel burned-out. *Rejuvenated* and *renewed* are two words that mean refreshed. It's wonderful to find a way to relax when our feelings overwhelm us. God promises to "refresh the weary and satisfy the faint." He provides many ways for us to find refreshment. What makes you feel refreshed? When you feel all-overish, heavyhearted, or burned-out, how can you make yourself feel better? Hanging out with friends and forgetting your worries for a while will help. So will spending time with God. If your feelings need some turning around, see if you can find ways to refresh them.

Lord, I could use some refreshment today. My feelings aren't in the best place right now. Please guide me to turning them around. Help me to feel refreshed, rejuvenated, and renewed. Amen.

Fascinated, Interested, Intrigued

For as he thinks in his heart, so is he.
PROVERBS 23:7 NKJV

Oriana felt fascinated by rap songs because she was interested in words that went together like poetry. She felt intrigued—curious—to find out if she could write rap songs and perform them too. Oriana listened to many rap songs, trying to learn how performers matched their words to the beats. As she listened, she noticed some bad language. The words seemed to fit with the beat, though, and Oriana wondered if it was okay to use them if the words fit the song. Proverbs 23:7 warns us to protect our hearts from any thinking that doesn't agree with God's. God wants us to feel fascinated by and interested in many things but not those that pull us away from Him, like rap songs with bad language. Do you think Oriana could create rap songs that glorify God?

Heavenly Father, I feel interested and curious about many things. There are some I would like to try, but only if they are okay with You. Please guide me away from those that intrigue me but wouldn't be pleasing to You. Amen.

I Feel Satisfied

I am not saying I need anything. I have learned to be happy with whatever I have.
PHILIPPIANS 4:11 NLV

Ava always wanted more. More stuff, more friends, more freedom, more love. She never felt satisfied—pleased with what she had. The more Ava thought about what she didn't have, the less grateful she felt for God's blessings. Had she turned her thoughts to the many ways God blessed her, that ugly feeling of not being satisfied would have gone away. God provides us with exactly what we need but not always what we want. Jesus' follower Paul wrote in Philippians 4:11 that he had learned to be happy with whatever he had. Paul had very little, but still he felt grateful. Paul's gratefulness led him to feel satisfied. It's okay to ask God for what you need. The Bible says to pray and bring our requests to God. But when you ask, remember to ask with thankfulness (Philippians 4:6).

Dear God, You know all my wants, and You always provide what I need. I feel satisfied and grateful for all You have given me. Amen.

Sometimes getting rid of
weighty feelings requires
help from someone else.
Don't be afraid to ask for help.

Weigh Those Feelings

*The LORD detests dishonest scales,
but accurate weights find favor with him.*
PROVERBS 11:1 NIV

Rarely do our feelings balance perfectly, but we can try to get them balanced enough that we feel content and at peace. A balance scale is a device with two sides that compare what things weigh. If you wanted both sides to weigh the same, you would add or take away from one side until the scale balanced. We can imagine weighing our feelings that way. Ugly feelings are heavy, and they put the scale out of balance. To get it to balance again, we have to get those ugly feelings to weigh less. To do that, we can spend time doing something we enjoy, think positive thoughts, and take a break to talk with the Lord. Sometimes getting rid of weighty feelings requires help from someone else. Don't be afraid to ask for help. It's important to take good care of yourself and keep your feelings balanced.

Father, help me to recognize when my feelings are out of balance. Lead me to get rid of the ugly feelings and replace them with something good. Amen.

God is for Me

What can we say about all these things?
Since God is for us, who can be against us?
ROMANS 8:31 NLV

Kathy's youth group at church was discussing a crime in their city that had left them feeling worried and afraid. Their leader encouraged them to share their feelings. Kathy felt better after sharing hers. She discovered that they all had one big worry: What if that happened to me? "What if that *did* happen to you?" their leader asked. Most kids responded with how they might feel. "But what would you *do*?" The leader asked. "Would you stay strong? Would you trust God?" Then he said, "For the next week, I want you to repeat Romans 8:31 whenever you feel worried or afraid: 'Since God is for us, who can be against us?' At our next meeting, let's see if repeating that verse changes your feelings." Imagine you were in Kathy's youth group. Whenever you feel worried or afraid, repeat Romans 8:31. Notice how your feelings change.

Dear God, I trust You. Since You are for me, no one can be against me. Amen.

I Feel Optimistic

We know that God makes all things work together for the good of those who love Him and are chosen to be a part of His plan.
ROMANS 8:28 NLV

When Kathy thought about Jesus always being on her side, loving her and caring for her, she felt less worried. She knew if trouble came, Jesus would be there to guide and help her. That gave Kathy a feeling of peace. Instead of worrying about all the bad things that might happen, Kathy shifted her thoughts to believing that with Jesus on her side, everything would be all right. Kathy memorized Romans 8:28, and before long she noticed her feelings shift from negative to positive. She felt optimistic—hopeful. Romans 8:28 reminds us that God works everything out for the good of those who love Him. He has a purpose for our lives, and His plans for us are good. If you haven't memorized Philippians 4:8, go back to page 10 and read it again. It lists things you can think of to make your optimistic feelings grow big and strong.

Father, I feel optimistic, knowing that You will work everything out for good. Amen.

I Feel Sorry

Tell your sins to each other. And pray for each other so you may be healed. The prayer from the heart of a man right with God has much power.
JAMES 5:16 NLV

We feel sorry when we regret something we did. It's an uncomfortable feeling. To get rid of it, we need to admit our wrongdoing and apologize. Sometimes that means saying "I'm sorry" to a person for what we did. But more often, it means saying "I'm sorry" to God. Believing that He will always forgive us helps make our sorry feelings go away. There is another kind of sorry feeling. We can feel sorry—sad—for someone's trouble. It is a feeling that shows we care. Can you think of a time when you felt sorry for someone? Did that feeling lead you to do something nice to show them you cared? Whether you feel sorry for something you did or sorry for someone's trouble, pray about it. Your prayer connects with God's power, and He is always ready to help or forgive.

Dear God, guide me to be sorry for my mistakes and to care for those who have trouble. Amen.

I Feel Generous

Each of you should give what you have decided in your heart to give, not reluctantly or under compulsion, for God loves a cheerful giver.

2 CORINTHIANS 9:7 NIV

Valeria's mom volunteered at church, bringing free meals to those in need. While Valeria was on spring break, her mom insisted Valeria come with her. "Do I have to?" Valeria complained. She already felt bored, and delivering meals sounded *really* boring. At church Valeria helped her mom pack the hot meals into their car. She wanted to wait in the car while her mom delivered each meal, but her mom said no. They gave meals to people who were old, sick, and disabled. At each stop, when she saw how grateful people were, Valeria felt happiness growing inside her heart. Going with her mom that day helped Valeria build up another good feeling—generosity. Later she and her mom talked about other ways Valeria could be generous. Soon Valeria was giving to others in many ways, and she always gave with a caring and cheerful heart.

Heavenly Father, I feel generous. Teach me to use my generosity to bring care and joy to others. Amen.

I'm Bored

Turn away from the sinful things young people want to do. Go after what is right. Have a desire for faith and love and peace.
2 TIMOTHY 2:22 NLV

Tanya's older brother spent all his free time playing video games and getting into trouble with his friends. Tanya cared about his feelings, and when she asked about them, he would usually answer, "I'm bored." When she suggested he practice on his keyboard, something he was good at, he felt irritated. "I don't want to!" he said. "Why don't you read a book or help clean the garage?" she suggested. Her brother looked at her and laughed. "That's boring!" he said. "Go away." Tanya wanted her brother to turn his ugly feelings around. She worried that feeling bored would get him into trouble. As she continued caring about his feelings, she prayed, asking God to help her brother get rid of his bored, ugly feelings and instead do something good. What do you most often do when you feel bored? Do you think it pleases God?

Dear God, when I have free time and feel bored, guide me to do something helpful and good. Amen.

A Bittersweet Feeling

What more could I have done for my vineyard? I hoped for sweet grapes, but bitter grapes were all that grew.
ISAIAH 5:4 CEV

Tanya was hopeful that her brother's feelings would change, but he continued feeling bored and getting into trouble with his friends. Then what Tanya had worried about most happened. Her brother got into serious trouble with the police. Tanya's hope turned into a bittersweet feeling. Bittersweet is when we have both sad and pleasant feelings at the same time. Tanya felt sad that her brother had messed up. Still, she had pleasant memories of the kind and caring brother he had been when Tanya was little. She used those good feelings to help boost her feelings of hope. Tanya continued hoping that her brother would turn his life around and live to please God. When something happens to make us feel sad, God gives us good thoughts too—good thoughts to help ease our ugly feelings.

Heavenly Father, when I feel sad about someone, please give me good thoughts of them. Help me to use those good thoughts to make the sadness go away. Amen.

My Best Friend

"I call you friends, because I have told you everything I have heard from My Father."
JOHN 15:15 NLV

The New Testament in the Bible begins with four books: Matthew, Mark, Luke, and John. Together they are called the Gospels. They tell the story of Jesus' life on earth from His birth to when He died on the cross for our sins, rose from the dead, and went back to heaven to be with God, His Father. Jesus is still with us in spirit. He wants to help and guide us. He understands us because when He was on earth, Jesus experienced many of the same feelings we have—sadness, joy, anger, tiredness, compassion, kindness, frustration, suffering, and more. Jesus wants to be your best friend. He loves you, and He wants to teach and guide you. If you trust Him, Jesus will help with every ugly feeling you have. He will make you strong so you can handle any obstacles that get in your way. You can trust Jesus to help you with everything.

Dear Jesus, You are my best friend. I can always count on You to love me and help me. Amen.

"I call you friends, because I have told you everything I have heard from My Father."

With All Due Respect

*Show respect to all men. Love the Christians.
Honor God with love and fear. Respect
the head leader of the country.*
1 PETER 2:17 NLV

Respect means always being polite. God made each of us as one of a kind. We have our own beliefs, opinions, and ways of doing things. When people accept us just as we are, we feel respected. We might not always agree with someone's beliefs, opinions, customs, or choices, but we should always show them respect by being polite, especially when we disagree. The Bible teaches us to respect everyone. Showing respect is one way we honor God. Everyone deserves respect. When we feel respected, we feel more confident, cared about, and loved. We feel safe around those who respect us because we know they will help, love, and care for us no matter what. Think about the way you treat others, especially those you disagree with. Do you show them respect by always being polite?

Dear God, when I disagree with someone, I sometimes feel frustrated and angry. Remind me that everyone deserves respect. Help me to react respectfully by being polite. Amen.

I Feel Disrespected

He who speaks strong words to a man will later find more favor than he who gives false respect with his tongue.
PROVERBS 28:23 NLV

Abigail's friend Lauren didn't believe in God, and she made fun of Abigail when she talked about her faith. Her disrespect left Abigail feeling hurt and angry. She had done her best to treat Lauren respectfully when they disagreed. She had to decide. Should she go on feeling disrespected, or should she tell Lauren how she was feeling? Abigail decided to share her feelings. "Lauren," she said, "it hurts me when you make fun of my faith in God. I know you don't believe in Him. I wish you did. But I have always been polite and respectful of your feelings. Will you please be respectful of mine?" Abigail's words were strong but still polite. When someone disrespects us, we can be polite and still stand up for our feelings and beliefs. If someone disrespects you, ask God to give you the right words to say.

Father, when I feel disrespected, help me to stand up for my feelings with words that are strong yet polite. Amen.

Sensitive Feelings

Be gentle and kind. Do not be hard on others. Let love keep you from doing that.
EPHESIANS 4:2 NLV

Our feelings are sensitive, easily hurt. The words people say and the ways they treat us can leave us feeling tearful and sad. It's important not to become so sensitive that we live most of the time with ugly feelings. We should remember that we deserve respect, care, and love. The company we keep makes a difference. When we surround ourselves with people who are gentle, caring, and kind, our feelings will get hurt less often. And when our feelings do get hurt, it is those people who will love us, build us up, and help us get rid of the ugliness so we can feel good again. Who are the people you can count on to be gentle with your feelings, caring, and kind? How does the way they treat you make you feel?

Dear Lord, when someone hurts my feelings, please remind me that I have family and friends who love me. They care about how I feel—and so do You! Amen.

I Am Sensitive

Do you have loving-kindness and pity for each other?

PHILIPPIANS 2:1 NLV

Sensitive isn't only a feeling. It also describes our attitude toward how others feel. When we notice how people feel, we can be sensitive to their feelings and act with kindness and caring. We can help them turn their feelings from ugly to good. Wendy was that kind of girl. She noticed how her friends felt, and when their feelings turned ugly, Wendy had a way of making things brighter. She always had kind words and compliments. She was a good listener. Wendy's positive attitude could make things seem less depressing and dark. Her sense of humor was often just what a friend needed to lighten the mood. And Wendy's smile lit up the room. Are you like Wendy—sensitive to how others feel God put inside your heart special ways for you to be sensitive. What about your personality can help people turn their feelings from ugly to bright?

God, please build up my sensitivity toward the way others feel. Guide me to show kindness and caring with my actions and my words. Amen.

Joyful Friendship

Then give me true joy by thinking the same thoughts. Keep having the same love. Be as one in thoughts and actions.
PHILIPPIANS 2:2 NLV

Social media is one way people connect, but it is even better and more rewarding to be social. It means you enjoy being around people. It is fun meeting people and getting to know them. The more people you meet, the more likely you are to have many friends. But friendship isn't about how many friends you have. It's about finding good friends who share your values. Friends who share your faith in God will bring you joy. You can feel comfortable talking with them about Jesus and doing fun activities you know God will approve of. Friends who love Jesus will know to treat you well and build up all your good feelings. You will find joy too by caring for them and showing them your loving-kindness. It's fine to have many friends, but keep those who share your values and faith in God closest to you. Those friends are like gold.

Heavenly Father, lead me to good Christian friends who share my faith and values. Amen.

I Feel Shy

For God did not give us a spirit of fear. He gave us a spirit of power and of love and of a good mind.
2 TIMOTHY 1:7 NLV

Camila felt shy. She didn't feel comfortable around many people, so she kept to herself. She wanted to make friends, join the dance team, and take an art class, but shyness kept her from trying. It stole her feelings of happiness and joy. The Bible says that God didn't create us with fear inside our hearts. Fear helps shyness grow. Fear says, "What if I'm not accepted? What if I fail?" Shyness is an ugly feeling. It pulls us away from wonderful experiences and making good friends. God gives us power to push away shyness. If you are like Camila and shyness is growing inside your heart, use the power God gave you. Be brave. Be bold. Join that dance team, art class, or whatever fun thing you've been dreaming of. You're going to love it!

Lord, I know that shyness is stealing experiences that could make me happy. Please give me power to push shyness away so I can follow my dreams. Amen..

PSALM 68:6

[God,] You find families for those who are lonely.

I Feel Lonely

[God,] You find families for those who are lonely.
PSALM 68:6 CEV

Camila's shyness made another feeling grow—loneliness. It grew big inside Camila's heart. Instead of exploring new activities and making new friends, Camila spent her time alone. She sometimes hung out with her younger siblings, but they didn't share her interests. Camila's loneliness felt like a deep, empty hole. God finds families for those who are lonely. A family isn't always made up of relatives. It can be made up of people who share similar ideas and care about each other. To get rid of her loneliness, Camila took a big step forward. She joined a youth group at a nearby church. Soon she felt part of a welcoming church family who cared about her, and the friends she made there filled up that big empty space inside her. If you feel lonely, ask God to help you find a family of friends where you'll fit in and feel accepted and loved.

Dear God, I hate this lonely feeling. I'm ready to send it away. Please lead me to the family of friends You have already chosen for me. Amen.

I Have Faith

Faith makes us sure of what we hope for and gives us proof of what we cannot see.
HEBREWS 11:1 CEV

Camila had faith that God keeps all His promises. If He promised to find a family for those who felt lonely, then He would do it! Before Camila joined the youth group, she had spent weeks talking with God, asking him to find a group of friends where she would fit in. Although she couldn't see God at work, Camila hung tightly to her strong feeling of faith. She trusted that God was working on her request. The Bible says faith can move mountains (Matthew 17:20). When we trust in God to love and help us, He can move those mountains of loneliness, fear, and sadness that keep us from enjoying life. Do you have faith in God to keep His promises? Grow that faith. Even when you can't see God working on your needs, trust that He is.

Heavenly Father, faith can be difficult sometimes, especially when I can't see answers to my prayers. But I will grow my faith strong, and I will keep trusting You. Amen.

I Feel Prayerful

I call to You from the end of the earth when my heart is weak. Lead me to the rock that is higher than I.
PSALM 61:2 NLV

Do you pray every day? Prayer is like plugging something in to make it work. Prayer plugs you into God's mighty power. The Bible says to pray about everything (Philippians 4:6). When big, ugly feelings like fear, sadness, anger, and loneliness are growing inside your heart, you might feel the Holy Spirit telling you to pray. If you can't think of the words to pray, you can ask the Holy Spirit to pray for you. The Bible says He will (Romans 8:26). You can also pray the words Jesus taught us to pray. You will find them on the next page. Tell God about your big, troubling feelings. Ask Him to help you get rid of them and replace them with feelings of peace, comfort, and joy. If you don't receive an answer right away, keep praying. Ask God to give you patience while He works on your requests.

Dear God, when I can't find the words, please help me to pray. Amen.

The Lord's Prayer

Never stop praying.
1 THESSALONIANS 5:17 NLV

When you can't find the words, you can always pray this prayer. This is how Jesus taught people to pray.

> *"Your Father knows what you need before you ask Him. Pray like this: 'Our Father in heaven, Your name is holy. May Your holy nation come. What You want done, may it be done on earth as it is in heaven. Give us the bread we need today. Forgive us our sins as we forgive those who sin against us. Do not let us be tempted, but keep us from sin. Your nation is holy. You have power and shining-greatness forever. Let it be so.'"* (Matthew 6:8–13 NLV)

Father in heaven, You know all my feelings. You know what I need even before I ask. Thank You for teaching me to pray and for the Holy Spirit who prays for me when I can't. Amen.

God's Word

All Scripture is inspired by God and is useful for teaching, for showing people what is wrong in their lives, for correcting faults, and for teaching how to live right.
2 TIMOTHY 3:16 NCV

Camila's youth pastor gave her a Bible that was easy to understand. She enjoyed studying the Bible and discussing it with her youth group friends. As she read, Camila discovered stories about people who shared her same feelings. Moses, for example, felt shy. Gideon felt afraid. Job felt lonely and depressed. Peter felt guilty. Reading the Bible helped Camila feel nearer to God. It built her feelings of faith and trust. She learned about God's great love, His faithfulness, and how she could live right to please Him. Do you read the Bible? There are Bibles written for girls your age that are easy to understand. Reading the Bible will help with your feelings and lead you nearer to God.

Dear Lord, sometimes I find the Bible hard to understand. Please help me find a Bible that meets my needs. I want to learn more about You and how You helped people with feelings like mine. Amen.

A Powerful Connection

Moses said to the Lord, "Lord, I am not a man of words. I have never been. . . . I still am not. For I am slow in talking and it is difficult for me to speak."
EXODUS 4:10 NLV

God chose Moses to free the Israelites from being held as slaves in Egypt. God told Moses to speak to Pharaoh, Egypt's leader, and tell him "God says, 'Let my people go!'" Moses felt shy. He felt afraid to do what God asked. Moses begged God to send someone else. But God wanted to send Moses. After much encouragement from God, and God allowing Moses to take his brother, Aaron, with him, Moses felt strong enough to speak to Pharaoh. With God's power helping him, Moses became a great leader. He led the Israelites out of Egypt and to a new land. Someday you might feel God leading you to do something big, something you feel afraid to do. Remember Moses. Don't give in to your feelings. Connect to God's power. Do what He asks and be brave.

God, I want to go wherever You lead me. Help me not to feel afraid. Amen.

A little love, please

"For God so loved the world that He gave His only Son. Whoever puts his trust in God's Son will not be lost but will have life that lasts forever."
JOHN 3:16 NLV

Camila had felt lonely, shy, and afraid, but participating in her church youth group helped chase those ugly feelings away. Camila became more aware of how many people loved her—her family, friends, and, most of all, God. She realized that God had blessed her with the greatest gift ever—Jesus! He promised to be with her throughout her life, and as Camila built up her faith and trust in Him, she knew that all the ugly feelings in the world would never be too much for Jesus to handle. He would stay with her and help her because she trusted Him as God's Son. Even when she died, Jesus would still be with Camila. She would live in heaven forever with Him and with everyone else who loved Him. Whatever you are feeling today, Jesus knows about it. He loves you, and He will bring you through it.

Jesus, thank You for living with me and filling my heart with Your love. Amen.

A little Joy, Please

"He will yet make you laugh and call out with joy."
JOB 8:21 NLV

Joy can be a big, happy feeling. "Yay! Hooray! Yippee! Bravo! Hallelujah!" In the Bible, we read about people clapping and shouting with joy, praising God. They shouted a joyful "Hosanna!" when Jesus rode on a donkey into the city of Jerusalem. Joy can also be a quiet, settled feeling. Jesus' follower Paul found joy in the middle of all kinds of trouble. He suffered greatly in prison. Still, Paul felt a quiet ongoing joy in his heart because he loved Jesus and Jesus loved him. Paul wasn't going to let any ugly feeling steal his joy. Instead, he held on to a quiet joyful attitude, always focusing on good things. It brought him much joy in prison, knowing that other Christians were spreading the word that Jesus had come to save us from sin. Joy can be a quiet feeling but a big one. When you have true joy, nothing can steal it away.

Lord Jesus, knowing You and feeling Your love inside my heart brings me joy. Amen.

Create Something!

"The Lord has filled him with the Spirit of God. . . . So he can make plans for working in gold, silver and brass, and cut stones to be set, cut wood, and do good work of every kind."

EXODUS 35:31–33 NLV

Anika didn't like talking to others about the big, ugly feelings she held inside. She talked about them to God though, and He reminded her of a special talent He had given her. Anika felt Him urging her to create something. So, instead of sitting in her room feeling angry and sad, Anika made art. She noticed that her ugly feelings were coming out with the images she drew and the colors she chose. She added some bright colors to make her art more cheerful. Creating something helped Anika to feel better. It made her ugly feelings feel not so big. There are many ways of being creative. Which are your favorites? Try expressing yourself through your creativity. See if it helps how you feel.

Dear God, thank You for inspiring me to express my feelings by being creative. Guide me to create something that shows how I feel. Amen.

Get Out of My Way!

With your help I can attack an army.
With God's help I can jump over a wall.
PSALM 18:29 NCV

Satan loves stealing good feelings, and he is great at slipping ugly feelings into our hearts and then blocking their way to get out. Watch out for him. Watch out, but don't allow fear to keep you from standing up to him and saying, "Get out of my way!" Jesus' follower James said, "Give yourselves to God. Stand against the devil and he will run away from you" (James 4:7 NLV). With God's help, you can attack Satan and his army, and they will run from you. You can take back any feelings Satan stole from you and keep ugly feelings out of your heart. With God's help, you can manage all your feelings and end up with most of them being good. You are a soldier in God's army, and He will give you everything you need to fight and win.

Dear God, when Satan tries to steal my good feelings, I trust You to give me courage to stand up and bravely shout, "Get out of my way!" Amen.

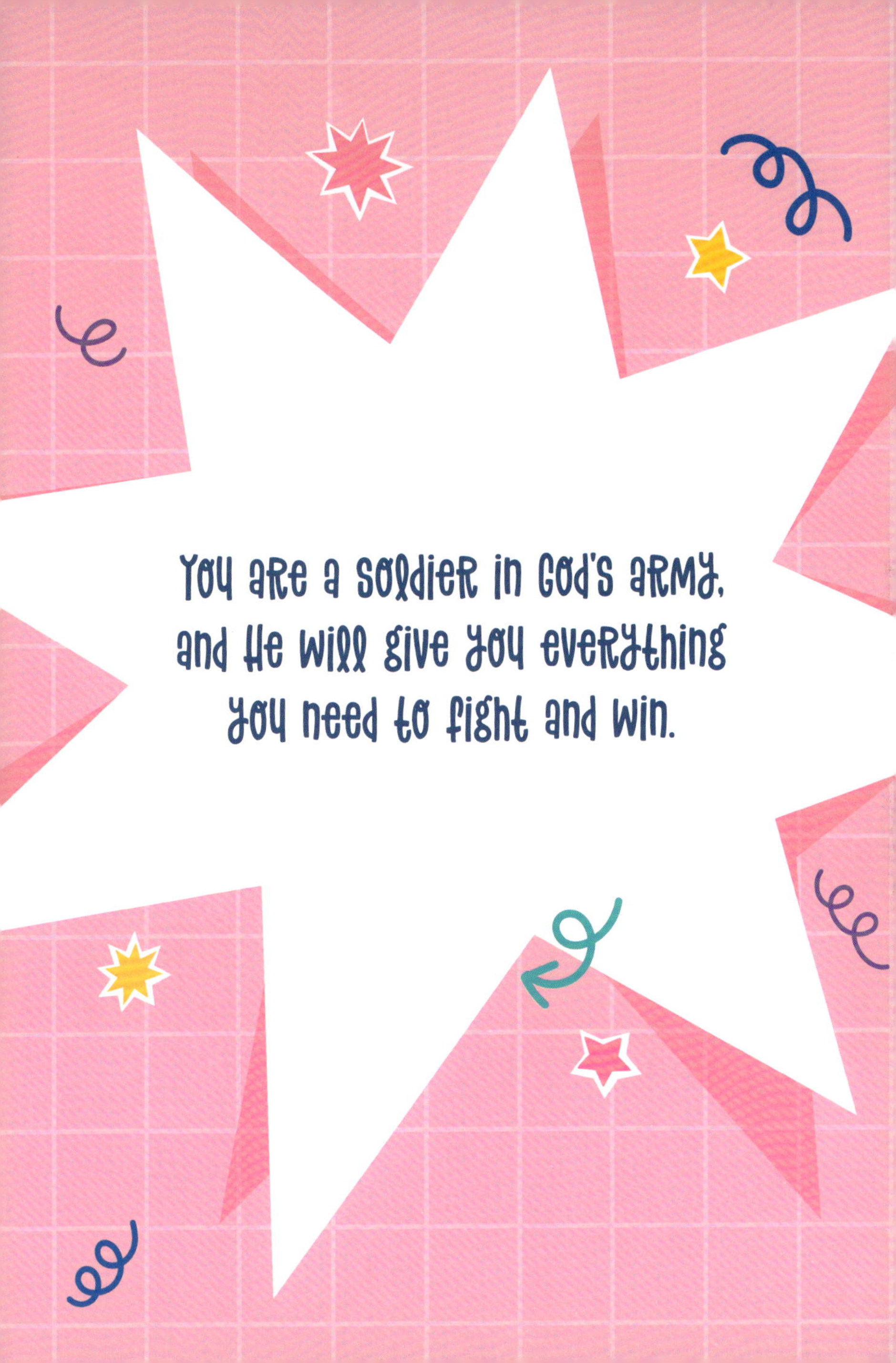
You are a soldier in God's army,
and He will give you everything
you need to fight and win.

A Text Mess

"Be careful or anger will tempt you to laugh at the truth."
JOB 36:18 NLV

Ruthie and her sister Sylvia had an argument in the morning before they left for school. Sylvia was in high school, and she was in charge of her younger sister after school until their mom came home. Sylvia could be bossy. "Come right in the house when you get home," she told Ruthie. "Don't stay outside playing with your friends." After school, while Ruthie was on the school bus, she got a text from Sylvia: "I locked myself out of the house." Ruthie answered with a laughing emoji. Sylvia responded with an angry emoji, and that started a string of not-so-nice texts. By the time Ruthie got home, both girls felt angry with each other and weren't speaking. Use what you have learned about feelings to decide how the girls might have avoided feeling angry. How could their behavior have been more pleasing to God?

Dear God, thank You for reminding me not to let out my anger toward others by laughing at them or using unkind words. Help me to stop disagreements before they start. Amen.

When Feelings Get Stuck

Jesus said, "God can do things men cannot do."
LUKE 18:27 NLV

Hurt and anger were stuck inside Amy's heart. A girl at school had hurt Amy's feelings. It happened months ago, but whenever Amy thought about it, it still stung. The anger and hurt she felt wouldn't go away. Amy prayed about it, but so far the feelings were still with her. One day Amy's grandma said, "Maybe it would help to forgive the girl. Forgiving her in your heart doesn't mean that you have to be friends with her. Pray about it. See what God says." Amy began asking God to help her forgive, and little by little, the hurt and anger went away. When big feelings get stuck inside, God knows how to get rid of them. This time He led Amy's grandma to help. If you have big feelings like anger, hurt, and sadness stuck inside, ask God to show you what to do. Ask Him to lead you to people who can help.

Father, I don't want these bad feelings stuck inside me. Show me what to do so I can let them go. Amen.

A One-Word Prayer

Help, Lord!
PSALM 12:1 NLV

When King David was a boy, not much older than you, he fought a huge enemy soldier named Goliath. All the Israelite men were afraid of Goliath because of his size, and they ran away. But young David stayed and faced the huge man. David knew the battle wasn't his but the Lord's, and David was sure God would help him. So, knowing that God was on his side, David charged head-on toward Goliath, and with just a slingshot and a stone, he knocked that giant man down. David's story reminds us not to run from our feelings but to face them head-on instead. Imagine any big, scary feeling as your Goliath. Will you run from it or face it bravely? God is on your side. All you need is this one-word prayer: "Help!" God will give you strength to face that huge feeling and knock it down.

Help! God, I'm facing a big, scary feeling.
I need to be brave so I won't run away.
Give me Your power to stay here and fight,
and I will knock this big feeling down. Amen.

More or Less?

Jesus stopped and called them. He asked,
"What do you want Me to do for you?"
MATTHEW 20:32 NLV

You've learned that feelings can be big, small, and every size in between. Some are beautiful. Some are ugly. Feelings can grow, or they can shrink until they no longer exist. Some hang on and get stuck. You've discovered which feelings are good and which are not. And, best of all, you know that God is the one you can trust with your feelings. He will help you to grow the good feelings and get rid of those you don't want. You have so many feelings! Make a list of those you want more of. Then list those you want less of. Pay close attention to your feelings and talk with Jesus about them. If He asked, "What do you want Me to do for you?" what would you say about your feelings?

Dear Jesus, I have many feelings, and they change so quickly. I want You to help me sort them out. I want to keep the good ones and get rid of those that are ugly or stuck. Amen.

The Most Powerful Feeling

God's love has been poured out into our hearts through the Holy Spirit, who has been given to us.
ROMANS 5:5 NIV

God is pouring into your heart the most powerful feeling of all, His love. God's love for you is mighty and great. His love can conquer every ugly feeling and situation. The God who made you controls the universe, everything good that exists, what you see and what you can't see. Every good feeling and every good thing come from Him. God has always loved you, and He will love you forever. He doesn't want ugly feelings inside your heart, and you can count on His love to help you get rid of them. If you feel bad, run to God. If you feel good, worship and praise Him. Trust in God's love to make all your good feelings grow.

Oh, God. How great is Your love! Pour Your powerful love into my heart. Fill it so full of Your goodness that ugly feelings can't form roots and grow. Please increase my good feelings and guide me to use them to serve You and others. Amen.